BFI FILM CLASSICS

. . . .

Edward Buscombe
SERIES EDITOR

Cinema is a fragile medium. Many of the great classic films of the past now exist, if at all, in damaged or incomplete prints. Concerned about the deterioration in the physical state of our film heritage, the National Film and Television Archive, a Division of the British Film Institute, has compiled a list of 360 key films in the history of the cinema. The long-term goal of the Archive is to build a collection of perfect show-prints of these films, which will then be screened regularly at the Museum of the Moving Image in London in a year-round repertory.

BFI Film Classics is a series of books commissioned to stand alongside these titles. Authors, including film critics and scholars, film-makers, novelists, historians and those distinguished in the arts, have been invited to write on a film of their choice, drawn from the Archive's list. Each volume presents the author's own insights into the chosen film, together with a brief production history and a detailed filmography, notes and bibliography. The numerous illustrations have been specially made from the Archive's own prints.

Could scarcely be improved upon ... informative, intelligent, jargon-free companions
The Observer

... each manages to give a sense of the film in question as it unfolds, without falling back on tedious explanations. The background information is finely researched and gracefully communicated .
The Times Saturday Review

The BFI's excellent new Film Classics series
Literary Review

Cannily but elegantly packaged BFI Classics will make for a neat addition to the most discerning shelves
New Statesman & Society

BOUDU
SAVED FROM DROWNING
(BOUDU SAUVÉ DES EAUX)

....

Richard Boston

BRITISH FILM INSTITUTE

bfi

BFI PUBLISHING

First published in 1994 by the
BRITISH FILM INSTITUTE
21 Stephen Street, London W1P 1PL

British Library Cataloguing in Publication Data
A catalogue record for this book is available from the British Library

ISBN 0–85170–467–0

Designed by
Andrew Barron & Collis Clements Associates

Typesetting by
Fakenham Photosetting Limited, Norfolk

Printed in Great Britain by
The Trinity Press, Worcester

CONTENTS

. . . .

ACKNOWLEDGMENTS
. . . .

Many thanks to: Sue Bobbermein, Roma Gibson, Dawn King and Sue Law of BFI Publishing; the staff of the BFI's Library and Information Services; the Series Editor Edward Buscombe, and (in reverse alphabetical order) David Wilson, Ginette Vincendeau, Peter Graham and Marie-Claude Chapuis.

Centre: Michel Simon, right partly hidden: Jean Renoir

1
....

Bertrand Russell says that the first philosopher was Thales of Miletus in the sixth century BC. Thales, who thought that everything is made of water, was soon followed by Heraclitus of Ephesus, whose variation on the theme was that everything is in a state of flux. Since everything is in a state of flux, Heraclitus argued, you cannot step into the same river twice. Unless I have misunderstood him, Heraclitus took the argument only half the way: if you can't step into the same river twice it must be equally true to say that you can't step into the same river once.

In any case, Boudu challenges Heraclitus by stepping into the river (or throwing himself or falling into it) once at the beginning of the film and again at the end. Whether it is the same river, and whether it is the same Boudu – these are matters we will have to think about. We are already in deep waters.

As with stepping into rivers, you can't read the same book twice, or hear the same piece of music twice, or see the same film twice. Since (like everything else) we are in a state of flux, we are different people the second time – older, though not necessarily wiser, but better informed, and with knowledge which includes memory of the first experience.

I first saw *Boudu sauvé des eaux* in Paris in the early 1960s. The next time (which was only a couple of years ago – the film has not been shown all that often) I found the film to be different from what I had remembered. For one thing it was much richer.

The *Boudu* which I carried in my memory for some thirty years started with a tramp throwing himself off a bridge in Paris and being rescued by a Latin Quarter bookseller, Lestingois, who takes him into his house and cares for him. Boudu, the tramp, repays the good Samaritan with the basest ingratitude. It is not just his table manners that are appalling; his entire behaviour is atrocious. When Boudu is rebuked for spitting on the carpet, he hawks into one of the bookseller's rare leather-bound first editions instead. When told to clean his shoes, he applies the polish with his fingers and then wipes them on the bed-linen of the lady of the house. He not only seduces the housemaid but also Madame Bookseller herself. In general he is as totally, gloriously, uproariously and anarchically reprehensible as Harpo Marx.

The pressures of middle-class respectability are gradually brought to bear on him. Boudu is tamed. Boudu is shaved and shorn, he is cleaned up and put in a suit with collar and tie. Then he wins a large sum in a lottery, and is manoeuvred into marrying the housemaid.

At this point (when I first saw the film) I felt badly let down, as must everyone whose soul bears the slightest spark of rebellion. *We* may make compromises, but surely Boudu can rebel against respectability on our behalf. But no – he's going to sell out just like all the rest, and settle down with his wife and brats and they'll live in a little box made of ticky-tacky and they'll all think just the same.

Then, at the very moment of final self-betrayal (the wedding scene), Boudu upsets the apple-cart (actually it's a rowing-boat) and thereby escapes from the threatened life sentence in a bourgeois prison of domesticity and holy padlock, and floats off into the sunset, back to his old vagrancy, a free spirit once more.

That is more or less what I remembered, and in its essentials the summary is accurate. What I had not remembered was the framework. Aristotle says in the *Poetics* that a play has a beginning, a middle and an end. This statement of the crashingly obvious has irritated me ever since I was made to read the old bore for the Cambridge English Tripos. Now it irritates me because I see that he was right and I was wrong. I had remembered the *middle* of *Boudu* vividly but I had forgotten much of the end and almost all of the beginning. And this is strange because (I now realise) it is the beginning and the end that are distinctively and specifically Renoir's. The middle, which is roughly three-fifths of the film, comes from a stage play by René Fauchois. And it is in the beginning and the end, which are Renoir's, that the river runs.

2

....

Renoir's first experience of the cinema was early, not only in his life but also in that of the medium, the two being almost exactly contemporaneous. Various dates are given for the birth of the cinema. Edison demonstrated the Kinetoscope to the National Federation of

Women's Clubs on their visit to his laboratory in 1891, and showed it commercially in New York in April 1894. Some prefer Louis Lumière's Cinématographe of 1895 as the starting-point. Whichever of these dates you prefer, Jean Renoir was born in the middle of them, on 15 September 1894.

In 1897, when he was aged a little over two, his nanny Gabrielle took him to the Dufayel department store, where they saw a film. It was about a big river. Another of his early memories is of Essoyes in the Aube, where with a peasant boy called Godefer he enjoyed a *Wind in the Willows* existence, simply playing about in boats on the tributary of the Seine called the Ource.

He found this 'as wonderful as the rise of the Guignol curtain'. Guignol, which he had also seen with Gabrielle, is the French equivalent of Punch and Judy and (like the river) also comes into his films, notably in the introduction of *La Chienne*. Renoir's screen often reminds us of the rectangle of the easel picture of the kind his father Auguste painted, but also it is often the rectangle of the theatre's proscenium arch and of the Punch and Judy show. There are theatres, stages and sets in *Boudu*, *La Grande illusion*, *Les Bas-fonds*, *La Marseillaise*, *Le Carrosse d'or*, *French Cancan*, *Eléna et les hommes*, *La Règle du jeu* and *Le Petit Théâtre de Jean Renoir*.

Even when there is no theatre or stage involved, Renoir can give a feeling which is less film than theatre. I am thinking specifically of the scene in the park at the beginning of *Boudu* where the stationary camera is pointed at an expanse as flat as a stage, where people walk across from one side to the other or towards or away from the camera. The direction of the camera is closer to Laurel and Hardy than, say, Eisenstein.

In Renoir's early memories, recalled in *My Life and My Films*, screen, stage and river merged:

> A thing that has unquestionably influenced my development as a creator of films is water. I cannot conceive of cinema without water. There is an inescapable quality in the movement of a film which relates it to the ripple of streams and the flow of rivers. That is a clumsy way of describing a feeling. The truth is that the affinity between the film and the water is more strong and subtle

because it cannot be explained. Lying on the bottom of the skiff with Godefer, with the rushes brushing our faces, I had a thrill very near to what I feel when watching a film which moves me deeply. I know we cannot go back upstream, but I am free to relive in my own fashion the sensation of leaves stroking the end of my nose. For me that is what a good film is, the caress of foliage in a boat with a friend.

In his wonderful biography of his father, Renoir remembers punting with Paul Cézanne, the son of the painter.

There is nothing so mysterious as a river . . . Away from other human beings, lost in the overhanging foliage, fearful of breaking in on the sound of the water gliding over the weeds, we felt as if we were characters in a tale by Fenimore Cooper, whose writings Paul had introduced me to. We lay on our stomachs in the skiff, silent and motionless, our faces near the surface of the water, watching the movements of a large fish, which in turn was watching its prey.

Films of Renoir's in which rivers or water play an important part (often explicitly recognised in the title) include *La Fille de l'eau*, *Boudu sauvé des eaux*, *Une Partie de campagne*, *Swamp Water*, *The Southerner*, *The Woman on the Beach*, *Le Déjeuner sur l'herbe* and *The River*. It is perhaps not too far-fetched to see the train and the railway track in *La Bête humaine* as a variation of the image of the boat on the river. Gabin on the train could be another Jean on Vigo's *L'Atalante*. The use of the image varies, but the river, the railway track, the road and the unreeling spools of movie film all seem to belong to the same ribbon family.

An anthology could be made of the uses of rivers in art, especially literature. Sweet Thames, run softly . . . Where Alph the sacred river ran . . . Ol' man river . . . Mark Twain's Mississippi. *Three Men in a Boat* . . . Probably the best remembered words Scott Fitzgerald wrote are in the closing paragraphs of *The Great Gatsby*:

Gatsby believed in the green light, the orgastic future that year by year recedes before us. It eluded us then, but that's no matter –

tomorrow we will run faster, stretch out our arms further . . . And one fine morning –

So we beat on, boats against the current, borne back ceaselessly into the past.

This is very different from Renoir's view. He says in the passage quoted above, 'I know we cannot go back upstream'. In fact we *can* go back upstream. If we couldn't go back upstream the river traffic would be one-way, which it is not. Renoir's comment is true neither literally nor metaphorically, for what is memory if it is not going back upstream? And what would Renoir be without memory? What would any of us be without memory?

The river runs inexorably from source to the sea, as life does from birth to death. On the way we may have before us hope or dread, and behind us regret or nostalgia. Renoir's artistic temperament was mostly a sunny one, optimistic for the future, enjoying the present and remembering the past fondly, perhaps even sentimentally. There is a bit of Pangloss in Renoir.

When Renoir says 'I know we cannot go back upstream', he must be thinking of the words of his father which feature so prominently in his biography of Auguste: 'One is merely a cork. You must let yourself go along in life like a cork in the current of a stream. You have to follow the current. You swing the tiller over to the right or left from time to time, but always go in the direction of the current.'

Renoir's films very often give this feeling of going along like a cork on the stream, both in the way the films work and in the attitude to life they display. As with Shakespeare it seems as though Renoir takes his characters, puts them in a situation and lets them get on with it. He doesn't push them; he lets them flow with the current of their own lives. Small, chance incidents direct events this way rather than that way. If the dog Black hadn't spotted something in the distance and run away, would Boudu have thrown himself in the river? It was by pure chance that the bookseller Lestingois was looking out of the window with his telescope when Boudu threw himself in the water. It was chance that gave Boudu the winning lottery ticket. Was it by chance that Boudu upset the boat of the wedding-party or did he do it just a little bit accidentally-on-purpose? Then Boudu doesn't rejoin the wedding party: instead he resumes his original vagabond character. Surely this is a deliberate decision, though that is not the way the bookseller Lestingois explains it to his wife and to Anne-Marie (is she Boudu's bride, wife or widow?). Lestingois consoles her by saying that Boudu has gone with the flow (*au fil de l'eau*), an echo not so much of *La Fille de l'eau* as of Renoir *père*'s cork on the stream.

For an image to work, it must do so on the realistic level as well as metaphorically. Thus the storm in *King Lear* is the one in Lear's mind, and at the same time it is a very real storm, with real thunder, lightning, rain and gales. In the same way a Renoir river has symbolic meaning, but it is also a real river, one in which you can swim or boat or fish or drown, and on which the light flickers.

And Boudu doesn't jump into just any river. Renoir goes to some trouble to establish the specific locality. At the beginning of the film Boudu jumps into the Seine in the middle of Paris from the Pont des Arts, by the Latin Quarter, the Left Bank which is the artistic and intellectual centre of Paris. At the end, in contrast to that very urban, cultural and cerebral bit of river, the wedding party is floating down the Marne just outside Paris in a setting as pastoral as an Impressionist painting.

But to make this contrast between the working urban river and the holiday rural one is an over-simplification, and Renoir is rarely simple or simplistic. His Paris river has working boats like the ones in *L'Atalante*, but it also has pleasure boats – in fact when Boudu is rescued it is to a *bateau mouche* that he is first taken. Similarly, as we take in the bucolic setting at the end, when Boudu sits on the banks of the Marne sharing a crust with a goat, we hear a long blast from a factory siren, and in the long pan shot we see river banks that are beautifully filmed but are not in themselves particularly beautiful, with a rather hideous iron box-bridge, cranes, heaps of sand and gravel, factory chimneys and assorted industrial paraphernalia.

These two river scenes can be directly related to specific paintings. Auguste Renoir's 1872 painting of the Pont Neuf shows a scene of the bridge at an angle and from a height very much like the Pont des Arts (one bridge along) as seen from the upstairs window of Lestingois' house. But more than anything by Auguste Renoir, *Boudu* calls to mind two pictures by Seurat. Jean Renoir's father knew Seurat only slightly, but they exhibited together and Jean remembers Pissarro talking about Seurat's new painting technique. Through his father, Renoir was more familiar than most at the time with the work of that dazzling generation of artists. Seurat's socialism and his interest in the stage and circus would surely have made an especial appeal to Jean Renoir.

I have no evidence for this, but I would be surprised if Renoir didn't know Seurat's great pair of paintings of the Seine near Paris. The National Gallery's *Bathers at Asnières* has in the foreground a reclining man in a bowler hat of the kind which at the end of the film Boudu throws in the water. With the bowler-hatted man in the Seurat painting is a dog not unlike Boudu's Black. Asnières is a suburb outside Paris which would be a suitable place for the Boudu wedding party. Renoir's scene may have been shot on the Marne, the other side of town, but if so he has found a stretch of river which contains something very similar to the kind of industrial landscape in the background of the Seurat picture, where on the horizon there is an iron bridge and factory chimneys adding their smoke to the dull sky.

A small boat is sailing to the right of the Seurat picture towards a group of trees. These are the scene of the companion picture, *Un dimanche d'été à la Grande Jatte*, which is peopled by an altogether more upmarket lot than the proletarians of the Asnières painting. La Grande Jatte was a place for the fashionable or semi-fashionable or *demi-mondaine* to parade themselves and perhaps pick one another up. The park scene at the beginning of *Boudu* may be filmed in the Bois de Boulogne rather than La Grande Jatte, but the action is just the same as in the Seurat painting. Smart people are walking up and down with their children and their smart dogs. It is no place for a filthy tramp, and it is in precisely such an inappropriate setting that we first see Boudu.

In their pictures of and around Argenteuil the group of painters who came to be called the Impressionists captured not just the effects of light and shade on water, boats, trees and grass. They also caught a holiday world of young people eating, drinking, laughing and flirting – moustache-twirling young men wearing boaters and horizontally striped vests; young women with lovely complexions and figures, inviting lips and flirtatious parasols, all disporting themselves on the water or in the *guingettes*, the little countryside and riverside inns. Many of these people had hard lives. These were brief precious moments snatched from the weekly urban treadmill, but from those moments there comes an ideal of happiness that still enthrals us more than a century later. It was almost extinguished by the 1914–18 war, but its life was prolonged by Jean Renoir, both in his biography of his father and in his films.

The Impressionist painters shared this Arcadian vision with the writers. The example that comes immediately to mind is Maupassant's short story 'Une Partie de campagne' ('A Day in the Country'), of which Renoir made such an enchanting film. As a young man Maupassant (born 1850) was as enamoured of the Seine and Marne as the painters were in the 1870s. Maupassant spent his Sundays rowing on the river around Argenteuil, drinking, picking up girls (and also, sadly, the syphilis which drove him to madness and caused his early death). These years were, he said, the happiest of his life. He rented rooms on the river and went rowing day and night in his heavy skiff. In 'Mouche' he says that 'My great, my only, my all-absorbing passion for

Georges Seurat, *Bathers at Asnières*

ten years of my life was the Seine.' His translator, David Coward, has written:

> For Maupassant, the river was an exotic place of adventure but also a source of mystery. The river, and water generally, is the moody representative of nature, and he exploits its moods to demonstrate his view that civilisation is precarious and that mankind is but a step removed from base animality.[1]

The description does not fit Jean Renoir exactly, but (especially in *La Fille de l'eau*) it is close enough.

Not far downstream from Argenteuil is Médan, the home of Zola, who with Daudet, Turgenev, Edmond de Goncourt and Maupassant made up the 'groupe des cinq'. 'Boule de Suif' was Maupassant's contribution to *Les Soirées de Médan*, a collection of short fiction by various authors. Zola's work is connected to Jean Renoir's through the Zola films *Nana* and *La Bête humaine*. If only Renoir had made a film of

The river in *Boudu*

Zola's *L'Oeuvre*, a novel in which Renoir is anticipated in the descriptions of Paris, of riverside pastoral, and not only in the spirit of the narrative but also (as we shall shortly see) in the use of movement, where the moving camera and the writer can create fluid and fluent effects quite different from those of the static camera or framed easel painting. And in Claude Lantier – what a part that would have been for Jean Gabin or Michel Simon!

Auguste Renoir was a friend both of Zola and Cézanne, and Cézanne's son and Jean Renoir were to become lifelong friends. The friendship between Zola and Cézanne *père* went back to their schooldays in Aix-en-Provence, where they were inseparable. Claude Lantier, the main character of *L'Oeuvre*, is clearly based on Cézanne, and the character of Sandoz is Zola himself. The early part of the book, based on their childhood in Provence, has lyrical accounts of their days passed in camping, picnicking, reading and playing about on the banks of the little river Arc under the gaze of la Montagne Sainte-Victoire. But then (in *L'Oeuvre*) Claude comes to Paris, and the rules of Zola's novels decree that he is as doomed to failure, disaster and a sticky end as are all the other members of the Lantier family, from Nana to Jacques Lantier (the Gabin character in *La Bête humaine*). And so it is with the painter Claude Lantier, who fails as father, husband and artist and ends up killing himself in front of his masterpiece.

Cézanne was at the best of times a prickly character. He briefly acknowledged receipt of Zola's complimentary copy of the novel and that was the end of a friendship that had been of extraordinary intensity from childhood well into mature adulthood. They never corresponded again, or even met or spoke together again, though there were opportunities.

If the early chapters of the novel anticipate parts of Jean Renoir's *Le Déjeuner sur l'herbe*, the descriptions of the Seine and Marne could almost refer to parts of *Boudu*.

Between these two margins, one ablaze with light, the other gloomy with shadow, the spangled Seine flowed, cut across by the narrow stripes of the bridges. . . . Above the houses dark in shadow the towers of Notre Dame stood resplendent, as though freshly gilded. Booksellers' boxes were beginning to take over the parapets along the embankment; under an arch of the Pont Notre-Dame, a lighter laden with coal was straining against the powerful current.

And when Claude and Christine leave Paris they go to the Arcadian river: 'When the sunny weather returned, their life was one long succession of blissful days; the months went by in monotonous felicity . . . down grassy lanes, along the banks of the Seine.'

Most relevant to *Boudu* is the passage in which Zola not only describes the Seine in Paris more or less as it is seen in the film but also does it as a panorama, thereby anticipating in words the great pan shots that Jean Renoir was so fond of and so adept at. It is also worth remembering that the Pont des Arts is the one Boudu jumps from.

In the foreground immediately below them lay the Pont Saint-Nicholas with the low huts that housed the various shipping offices, the broad sloping wharf, its paving stones heaped up with sacks and barrels and sand; alongside, a string of loaded barges being swarmed over by a host of dock porters, and, stretched out over it all, the great iron jib of an enormous crane. Against the far bank, an open-air bath, gay with the shouts of the last of the season's bathers, flaunted the strips of grey tenting that served as its roof as bravely as if they were banners. Between the two the Seine, clear of all traffic, flowed along, greeny-grey, whipped up into little dancing wavelets tipped with white and pink and blue. The middle distance was marked by the Pont des Arts, with the thin line of its roadway, raised aloft on its network of girders, fine as black lace, alive with endless foot-passengers streaming perpetually to and fro like so many ants. Beneath it, the Seine flowed away into the ancient, rusty stone arches of the Pont Neuf, away to the left as far as the Ile Saint-Louis in one straight vista, bright and dazzling as a stretch of mirror. Higher again, much higher, higher than the twin towers of Notre Dame, now the colour of old gold, two spires rose; behind the towers, the cathedral spire, and on the left, the spire of the Sainte Chapelle, so fine, so graceful that they seemed to sway with the breeze.

It is hard not to think that Renoir had this passage in mind when making parts of *Boudu*.

3

·························

The Boudu wedding party floats off to the sound of a band playing Strauss's 'Blue Danube'. Claudio Magriz's *Danube* is a recent and major contribution to river literature. Early on in the book he discusses the centuries-old dispute over the precise whereabouts of the source of the great river, and speaks of Amadeo, the 'highly esteemed sedimentologist and secret historian of red herrings'. Amadeo finds the spring which is considered to be the source of the Danube but notices that the spring water itself comes from a sodden meadow a little further up the hill. But where did *that* water come from? He follows the rivulets up the hillside and comes to a shed where there is a gutter gushing water. And the water in the gutter comes from a basin which is always overflowing because no one has yet managed to turn off the tap. What would happen if someone did manage to turn off the tap? Would this turn off the Danube? Would Vienna, Budapest, Bratislava and Belgrade become waterless?

This is not the only problem. Magriz points out that at Passau the Danube meets the little river Ilz and the great river Inn. The Inn here is broader and deeper than the Danube and has run a longer course. Why then is the Danube not a tributary of the Inn? Why didn't Strauss write a waltz called 'The Blue Inn'? Magriz claims that the answer is: when two rivers mingle, the main stream is taken as being the one which forms the larger angle with the subsequent course.

I am as sceptical about that explanation as I am about the existence of Amadeo, even though I feel the sedimentologist and historian of red herrings to be a kindred spirit. If I have red-herringed in discussing Thales, Heraclitus, Seurat, Zola, Magriz and others, I am not repentant, and I will do so again. What I am trying to do, after my own fashion, is to examine sediment, look for sources and think about what is the main stream and what are the tributaries that went into the making of *Boudu*.

·························

In championing their *auteur* idea, the polemicists of *Cahiers du cinéma* hailed Renoir as the very model of a directorial supremo. This must have done wonders for Renoir's self-esteem because by that time he was getting on in years and feeling a bit neglected. He showed his gratitude to his young admirers by dedicating *My Life and My Films* 'to those film-makers who are known to the public as the "New Wave" and whose preoccupations are also mine'. In his Foreword he expands on this:

> In these days we recognise that film is the work of its maker, just like a novel or a painting. . . . The cinema of recent years has brought the acceptance of the idea that the maker of a film is the director. . . . Today we have films signed 'Truffaut' or 'Jean-Luc Godard' just as we have novels signed 'Simenon' or 'André Gide'.

Well, up to a point. Certainly we go to see a Hitchcock or a Kurosawa, but if I go to a Louis de Funès film it is because I find the actor Louis de Funès so funny: I haven't a clue who the director is. Without cheating, can you say off the top of your head who directed *Duck Soup* or any other Marx Brothers film?

Or take as an example *The Sweet Smell of Success*. Alexander Mackendrick's direction is superlative but it's not a one-man show. What makes it such a great film is that it brings together, with Mackendrick as director, the talents of Clifford Odets as writer, James Wong Howe's photography, the music of Elmer Bernstein and Chico Hamilton, and the acting of Burt Lancaster, Tony Curtis, Susan Harrison and Barbara Nichols. It is an achievement of cooperation.

Contrary to what Renoir says, a director's film can never be like a novel signed Simenon, or a painting signed Picasso. Writing and painting are solitary occupations. It is true that Simenon didn't make his own paper and typewriter, but otherwise a Simenon novel is all his own work. In elevating the director, the *cinéastes* of *Cahiers* almost seem to suggest that actors, photographers, musicians and others are no more than rude mechanicals on the level of Simenon's suppliers of paper and typewriter ribbons. Where, one wonders, would the New Wave directors have been without the photography of Raoul Coutard?

As it happens, I am writing these words a few days after Fellini died. Fellini literally put his name on his films – *Fellini Satyricon*, *Fellini Roma*, *Fellini's Casanova*. But even in a case as extreme as that of Fellini (which is extremely extreme), 'Fellini' was not Federico alone. He would have made wonderful art of some kind whatever he did, but the Fellini we know would have been very different without Rota's music and the acting of Giulietta Masina and Marcello Mastroianni.

The choice of Renoir as an exemplar of the *auteur* puzzles me. Renoir's talents were not dictatorial. It is true that he was active in every department from screenplay and direction to acting and editing, and he did put his name on one film, his last, *Le Petit Théâtre de Jean Renoir*, but what is more noticeable is the generosity with which he encouraged or enabled the work of others to flourish. Renoir's great strength was the opposite of doing everything himself. What he did was to get the best out of other people – writers, actors, cameramen, whoever.

The statement is attributed sometimes to Picasso, sometimes to T. S. Eliot, that minor artists borrow, great artists steal. Renoir was a great thief. He was a highly cultured man, with a huge knowledge of painting, literature, drama, music; he knew his Voltaire and Zola, his Racine and Beaumarchais, Marx, Robert Louis Stevenson, Gorky, Flaubert, Molière, Maupassant, Feydeau, Marivaux, Shakespeare. And he took from all of them. He took from his cameramen, he took from his actors and actresses, he took from anyone who could contribute, and in doing so (with, needless to say, his own huge artistic contribution) he was able to make a whole that was greater than the sum of its parts.

Renoir himself was well aware of this. He once declared himself so much in favour of plagiarism that he thought anyone found committing it should instantly be awarded the Légion d'honneur – thereby making more or less the same point as Eliot and/or Picasso. The great artist takes what he wants and makes it his own. As the son of a world-famous father, Jean Renoir was always aware of the question of the relative importance of heredity and environment, nature and nurture. He puts it well in the introduction to *My Life and My Films*, where he says: 'We do not exist through ourselves alone but through the environment that shaped us. Of course it would be an exaggeration to claim that a potato, planted in suitable conditions, would yield strawberries.'

The potter takes clay and makes it into whatever shape he wants; even so, much of the end result depends on the nature of the clay. An artist can't work without materials or material of some kind. The Danube would not be the great river it is were it not a confluence of tributary rivers. There is no tap that could turn off the Danube. There is no one source for *Boudu*, which is why it is so rich. It wouldn't exist without Renoir, but it also wouldn't exist without the contribution of Michel Simon (and I don't just mean that he financed the film, though he did). Nor could there be a *Boudu* without René Fauchois.

4

....

Throughout his career Renoir adapted the plays, novels and short stories of others and turned them into films which he stamped with his unmistakeable signature. His sources go from Maupassant (*Une Partie de campagne*), Gorky (*Les Bas-fonds*), Zola (*La Bête humaine* and *Nana*) and Flaubert (*Madame Bovary*) at the beginning of his career, to Prosper Mérimée (*Le Carrosse d'or*), Robert Louis Stevenson (*Le Testament du Dr Cordelier*, from *Dr Jekyll and Mr Hyde*) and Rumer Godden's *The River*.

When adapting other people's work for the screen, Renoir was capable of exercising as much latitude as Shakespeare, Eliot and Picasso did with their originals. With *Les Bas-fonds* Renoir took the lower depths from Russia and placed them on the banks of the Marne (with Gorky's approval). When he started on the script of *La Bête humaine*, he hadn't even read the novel. He said, 'I skimmed over it quickly, it seemed fascinating, and I said "OK, let's do it." We had to start straight away. I'm very proud of the following athletic feat: I wrote the script in twelve days, which isn't bad!' He moved the time from the nineteenth century to 1938, and changed crucial elements in the narrative. Yet, as with Gorky's play, he somehow remained faithful to the spirit of the novel. Kurosawa treated *The Lower Depths* in an equally free way. Without wanting to get into the whole subject of translation, I would suggest that (whether it is a matter of translation from one language to another or from one medium to another) in the hands of such artists this liberal treatment preserves the authenticity of the original more than any literal version ever could.

Gorky, Zola and most of Renoir's originals were great writers. By contrast René Fauchois' *Boudu sauvé des eaux* was what the French call a *boulevard* play. This is a rather contemptuous term for a piece of commercial theatre which in British terms would cover everything from West End drawing-room comedy to Whitehall farce. Renoir took this run-of-the-mill *boulevard* play and transformed it into a masterpiece. That, at least, is the account given by one writer after another in discussing this film.

It is true that Renoir changed the ending. In Fauchois' play Boudu and Anne-Marie get married and that's it, whereas Renoir's film ends with Boudu escaping from holy padlock and heading for a future of independent, vagrant liberty. Michel Simon had a flaming row with Renoir over the ending, and not only did the film belong to Simon in terms of hard cash (since he was the producer) but also Michel Simon was not someone one would care to have a flaming row with at any time. But Renoir's cherubic appearance contained a tough old nut, and a wily one. Simon wanted Boudu to settle down with Anne-Marie but spend his lottery winnings on something like a huge wedding party with thousands of tramps as guests. It could have made a terrific scene, or Simon could have made it a terrific scene, but Renoir suggested to him that if Boudu was returned to the wild, and if the film proved a financial success, then there could be Boudu sequels – perhaps as many as one a year. At any rate Renoir got his own way and his own ending.

Renoir said that as usual he had made a great many changes to the original story. 'Fauchois, the author, took this in very bad part and threatened to have his name removed from the credits.' But Fauchois was fair-minded and generous. Years after the film came out he saw it again and said (*Cinéma* 56, no. 7, November 1955) that when he first saw the film he had been over-possessive. *'J'ai souffert d'un complexe de paternité.'* His paternal possessiveness had made him unjustly misunderstand the film-maker's work. He now thought he had been wrong and asked Renoir to excuse him. 'I have just seen the film again and I admired it and am happy to say so. As a very free adaptation of my work, *Boudu* belongs to Renoir.' Fauchois said the film was the work of a master, that he approved of the ending, and that he was so carried away by the direction, the style, the rhythm and by Michel Simon that he found himself laughing at bits which (he had to remind himself) he had written himself. All in all Fauchois sounds as though he was a really nice man. He reminds me of someone. Who is it? Of course – it's the man who pulled Boudu out of the water, the bookseller Monsieur Lestingois.

René Fauchois was no mere hack. His career started as an actor with the Sarah-Bernhardt company, and indeed he acted the part of Lestingois in the stage *Boudu*. In a long career he wrote a great many plays, often in verse. Great musicians were a favourite subject: he did (among others) Beethoven, Rossini and Mozart. In 1919 Gabriel Fauré wrote the music for one of his stage productions, as did Reynaldo Hahn; and on 14 July of the same year Fauchois' *Boudu* opened in Lyon.

The play was produced in Paris the next year and was revived frequently. In 1925 Michel Simon played Boudu on stage, with Fauchois as Lestingois. What some will find surprising is that *Boudu* was on the Paris stage again the year *after* Renoir's film came out in 1932 and again in 1939. In fact the stage play was in almost constant production throughout the inter-war years.

So Fauchois' play was not some unconsidered trifle that Renoir picked up and dusted off. On the contrary, it was a long-running success. Nor was Renoir's film a case of a younger generation breathing new life into the work of an old fogey – Fauchois was a near contemporary of Simon and Renoir. But the received version is that Fauchois was merely a *boulevard* dramatist. Thus we find François Truffaut writing that *Boudu* is taken from 'a banal vaudeville play by René Fauchois'.[2] Truffaut says the play is *une pièce vulgaire et dépourvue d'intérêt*. Penelope Gilliatt calls it 'a minor play of the time', and Alexander Sekonske, Ronald Bergan and others make similar disparaging and condescending remarks.

They are all agreed that Renoir toughened the ending. Jacques Fanston writes: 'Michel Simon with Renoir transfigures the mediocre boulevardier play which inspired it.' Sesonske: 'Renoir's adaptation . . . transforms the film into an anarchic romp with Boudu at its centre, a work very far from the triumph of middle-class culture presented on the stage.' Ronald Bergan says that the film questions conventional bourgeois values, 'something the original play had little interest in doing'. Bergan also says that 'the Renoir film, which changed the slant of the original, was as far from the world of boulevard comedy as it could get, particularly the ending. In the play the anarchic tramp is reintegrated into society by marrying the maid; in the film, Boudu, on the wedding day, escapes at the last moment, regaining his untrammelled existence.' Some of these comments are so wide of the mark that it looks very much as though one writer has been following the other. It is hard to believe that any of them actually read Fauchois' play.

Fauchois' *Boudu sauvé des eaux* is a very witty play, full of ideas. If this statement is at all surprising it is because it goes so completely against the version propounded by Truffaut *et al*. Surely it would have been far more surprising if Renoir had chosen to film, and Michel Simon had chosen to act in and produce, a play as banal as Truffaut *et al*. make out. Having read it, I would very much like to see a stage production of a play which combines the farce of Feydeau with social comment and satire worthy of Shaw.

Before reading the play I wondered what I was going to find. What dross of Fauchois' would turn out to have been transformed into gold by Renoir? What in the film would turn out to be simply Renoir inventions, additions or embellishments? I thought of the moments in the film which seemed quintessentially Renoir. Boudu spitting into the volume of Balzac's *La Physiologie du mariage*, for example, was something which must surely have been thought up by Renoir, or by Renoir and Simon, or by Simon himself.

What else? Boudu eating the sardines with his fingers must be Renoir and/or Simon. Boudu refusing to wear a suit in the street because the children will laugh at him; Anne-Marie sticking her tongue out at Boudu; Boudu cleaning his shoes on the curtains and bed-covers; Madame Lestingois' description of Boudu as a troglodyte – surely none of these would be in Fauchois' play.

And there was one thing I knew for certain wouldn't be in the play. This was the mole (*grain de beauté*) on Madame Lestingois' left breast. It receives precisely the same erotic attention that is given to the small scar in exactly the same place on Elsa Andersen (Winna Winfried) in *La Nuit du carrefour*, which Renoir made in the same year as *Boudu*.

Had anyone been scoring, my predictions would have got precisely no points. All the above are in Fauchois' play, including

Madame Lestingois' mole (and incidentally the scar in *La Nuit du carrefour* is also in the Simenon novel on which it is based).[3]

Fauchois' stage play has one set, a domestic interior. This precludes the pastoral scenes at the beginning and end of the film, the prelude with the nymph and faun with pan-pipes being quintessentially Renoir. In fact they too are in the play, though in the dialogue. Lestingois says to Anne-Marie that she is like one of the nymphs the ancient poets used to celebrate. '*Tu es pareille aux nymphes que les anciens poètes ont célébrées.*' Like them she is *souple* and knows how to frolic in the forests, to drink from the fountain, and on a summer's night to dance naked by moonlight to the sound of pipes. Crowned with roses and myrtle, thyme in his hand, Bacchus would preside over the nuptial feast of Priapus Lestingois and Chloe Anne-Marie. A very pretty speech, which bowls Anne-Marie over.

Lestingois' view of marriage (of his own marriage anyway) is jaded. He says that long ago he married a pretty girl who was blonde and slim, who didn't talk much and who blushed charmingly. That person ceased to exist long ago. He hasn't changed: he's still interested in the golden nymphs, whereas Madame Lestingois is interested only in food. It is here (in play and film) that Anne-Marie says, 'Je vous aime, Monsieur Lestingois.' Whereupon Lestingois changes the subject and thinks of food. He tells Anne-Marie to be off to the kitchen and take care of the soup and don't forget the salt. Anne-Marie: 'I won't forget, even if I'm thinking about . . . tonight.' She leaves the bookseller musing to himself. 'My pipes are tired,' he says, 'and some shepherd will take her from me soon, with his new flute.'

Throughout the middle section of the film Renoir sticks fairly closely to Fauchois' action and dialogue. One variation is that in the play Lestingois is not with Anne-Marie but with his wife when he first observes the tramp while looking out of the window. He says that the tramp has *l'air sinistre.*

MME LESTINGOIS: The police shouldn't let people like that go about in broad daylight.
LESTINGOIS: Does that mean they should only be let out at night? I am more radical than you; I think we should get rid of the poor.

That exchange is pure Shaw. Later, when Boudu has provoked Madame into calling him a troglodyte – by leaving taps on, cleaning shoes on bed-linen, spitting and so on – Lestingois says, 'You can't do anything with people like that.'

> MME LESTINGOIS: That's what I said the first day.
> LESTINGOIS: You were right. One shouldn't rescue people of that sort.

This comment is usually taken as proof positive of the limits of Lestingois' liberalism and evidence that in the end his outlook is ineluctably bourgeois. The play (more than the film) shows that what the exchange is telling us about is the relationship between husband and wife. Lestingois always talks ironically to his wife, rather as Mr Bennett does in *Pride and Prejudice*; he picks on every utterance by the feather-brained women of his family and never misses the chance to make a sardonic or sarcastic remark which shows how stupid they are and by implication how intelligent and superior he is.

Are Jane Austen, Fauchois and Renoir ridiculing the women or are they exposing the cheap point-scoring of the males? Or both at once? The relevant point here, though, is that Lestingois always speaks ironically to his wife. Therefore when he says to his wife that one shouldn't rescue people like Boudu he means the opposite. People like Boudu are precisely the ones you do rescue. People like Lestingois don't need rescuing.

This point is if anything less clear in the film, which is centred on Boudu rather than Lestingois. In fact in narrative terms the major change by Renoir isn't so much in giving the story a different ending as in shifting the centre of attention from the character of Lestingois to that of Boudu. The change of ending is also important, though. At the end of the *play* the student to whom Lestingois gave the book enters to find Boudu, Anne-Marie and the Lestingois wife and husband all looking miserable. When the student and Lestingois are left alone together the student asks if something bad has happened.

> LESTINGOIS: Not yet, but it soon will.
> STUDENT: Really?
> LESTINGOIS: They're getting married.

That is by no means the happily-ever-after ending almost invariably attributed to the play. If anything, it is Renoir's ending that is upbeat. In Renoir's version, Boudu escapes. Fauchois' Boudu gets a life sentence, a marriage much like that of Lestingois.

5

There are cinema purists who dismiss Marcel Pagnol as a director whose films consist of no more than the result of sticking a camera in front of a performance of a stage play. There's some truth in this charge (if doing such a thing is an offence), but it doesn't alter the fact that a play like *Marius* is wonderful theatre; Raimu, Charpin, Fresnay and Orane Demazis act superbly, and the film has preserved those performances. It may not be cinema as understood by, say, Fellini but it's a record of something of real quality.

It is also true that Renoir is a very different animal from Pagnol. Although Renoir's films often refer to the theatre he is most certainly a maker of films, not a filmer of stage-plays. Renoir learnt his art in the silent cinema, the purest film of all, and whereas Pagnol would be almost nowhere without the crackling dialogue, Renoir could always tell a story, and comment on the action, in visual terms. (*The River*, which is like an extended visual metaphor, would in fact have benefited from having fewer words.)

Boudu is, as the credits say, '*D'après la pièce de René Fauchois. Réalisation de Jean Renoir.*' Behind the Renoir film (and not all that far behind) is the Fauchois play. I now want to suggest that behind the Fauchois play (and not all that far behind) is George Bernard Shaw's play *Pygmalion*, later to be translated into *My Fair Lady*. If I am right in this, the genealogist or Magriz source-searcher would have a family tree – or river and tributaries – that goes: *Pygmalion* (stage) → *My Fair Lady* (stage) → *My Fair Lady* (film); and *Pygmalion* (stage) → *Boudu* (stage) → *Boudu* (film).

Pygmalion was first performed in 1913, six years before the stage *Boudu*. Internal evidence strongly suggests that Fauchois knew Shaw's play. Higgins says of Eliza, 'It's almost irresistible. She's so deliciously low – so horribly dirty.' When Lestingois first sees Boudu he says,

'Look at that *clochard*. I've never seen such a perfect example.' Eliza is taken from the gutter, Boudu from the river. They are taken to comfortable middle-class homes and the first thing that happens is that they are stripped, scrubbed, cleaned and clothed. Then Higgins sets about turning Eliza into a member of the middle class, as does Lestingois with Boudu.

A difference is that in a way Boudu is both Eliza and her father Doolittle. Boudu, Eliza and her father are all completely ungrateful to their middle-class benefactors. Doolittle describes himself as being a member of the undeserving poor. Boudu and Doolittle both unexpectedly come into money, and both find themselves forced into a respectable marriage and faced with being got to the church on time.

Pygmalion was first performed in Paris at the Théâtre des Arts on 28 September 1923. Michel Simon was Doolittle. Shaw considered that the play was 'thrown away in Paris by maladroit handling' (Shaw's Letters, vol. 3, page 891). In a letter to Augustin Hamon (7 December 1923) he wrote that Paris 'can now boast of being the only city in the world where it has failed. That is not much consolation for us, unfortunately. But if theatrical people persist in regarding the play as a love affair between Higgins and Eliza, they deserve all they get in the way of failure.'

Whether or not *Pygmalion* is behind *Boudu*, there were people who were quick to claim that behind *Pygmalion* was Smollett's *Peregrine Pickle*, where in Chapter 47 'Peregrine sets out for the Garrison, and meets with a Nymph of the Road, whom he takes into Keeping and metamorphoses into a fine Lady.' Shaw was an indefatigable letter-writer, but so many people wrote pointing out the Peregrine–Pygmalion connection that on this occasion he wrote a standard letter for his secretary to send out. It is a useful comment on the issues I have raised about sources, tributaries, borrowings. The letter goes:

Dear Sir

Mr Bernard Shaw desires me to say that his attention has been called repeatedly to Peregrine Pickle since Pygmalion appeared. This is interesting as showing that people still read Smollett. He never read P.P.: Humphrey Clinker was his sole boyish excursion into Smollett. This is lucky as otherwise his play might have been prevented or aborted. The experiment of two writers of fiction treating the same subject and producing the same series of incidents – the same result practically – shews that the human imagination always runs in the same grooves, and that this is the explanation of almost all the alleged plagiarisms.

yours faithfully
Blanche Patch
Secretary

The first thing with both Boudu and Eliza is that they are taken off and washed and cleaned and clothed. In *Pygmalion*, the housekeeper Mrs Pearce says, 'Might I ask you not to come down to breakfast in your dressing gown, or not to use it as a napkin to the extent you do, sir. And if you could be so good as not to eat everything off the same plate, and to remember not to put the porridge saucepan out of your hand on the clean tablecloth, it would be a better example to the girl.' This is not unlike what Madame Lestingois says to Boudu. The difference is that in Shaw's play it is not Eliza but Mrs Pearce's employer Professor Higgins who is being rebuked for his appalling table manners.

Again, Lestingois quizzes Boudu about his morals, or the lack of them, in a way which was anticipated by the exchange between Pickering and Doolittle:

> PICKERING: Have you no morals, man?
> DOOLITTLE (*unabashed*): Can't afford them, Governor . . . I'm one of the undeserving poor: thats what I am . . . I aint pretending to be deserving. I'm undeserving and I mean to go on being undeserving. I like it, and thats the truth.[4]

Again, Liza's 'Why didn't you leave me where you picked me out of – in the gutter? . . . I wish you left me where you found me' is echoed by what are almost the first coherent words that Boudu utters: 'Why didn't you let me drown?' In the eyes of a Higgins or a Madame Lestingois (less so in the eyes of a Colonel Pickering or Mrs Pearce or Higgins's mother, or indeed Monsieur Lestingois), Liza and Boudu are both monsters of base ingratitude. But the way Liza and Boudu see it is that of the child against the parent. The parent says, 'You ungrateful so-

and-so, we gave you life, we gave you the best years of our lives, we gave you everything.' To which the child can quite reasonably reply, 'Why should I be grateful? I didn't ask to be born. It was your idea, not mine.' At one point Boudu tells Anne-Marie that he has never said thank you to anyone.

When Doolittle inherits money he says it has ruined him: 'Destroyed my happiness. Tied me up and delivered me into the hands of middle-class morality. It's making a gentleman of me I object to.' Boudu also comes into money, and is threatened by marriage and middle-class morality.

I will not go systematically through all the similarities between the Shaw play and that of Fauchois, but it is worth pointing out that the endings of both of them are thoroughly confusing. In a way that would now be called post-modernist Boudu (in the film) manages both to marry Anne-Marie and also not to. Fauchois himself was never satisfied with the ending of his play and was always tinkering with it (even adding a fourth act in which Boudu gets Madame Lestingois pregnant). Fauchois' fury may (understandably) have been exacerbated by the realisation that Renoir's ending was better than his own. Still, the play's original ending was a strong one, and Fauchois would have done well to leave it alone.

The ending of *Pygmalion* is if anything more mysterious. It is interesting that nobody seems able to remember quite how *My Fair Lady* ends, but the consensus is that Eliza comes in carrying Higgins's slippers. (Incidentally, Anne-Marie is another slipper-carrier. When she puts them on Lestingois, Boudu says, 'Can't he do that himself? Why are you doing it?' 'Because I want to,' she says, and sticks her tongue out at Boudu.) At the end of Shaw's play the only two characters on stage are Professor Higgins and his mother. The final stage direction reads: 'They kiss, Mrs Higgins runs out. Higgins, left alone, rattles his cash in his pocket, chuckles; and disports himself in a highly self-satisfied manner.'

In the afterword of the printed play Shaw comments:

> The rest of the story need not be shewn in action, and indeed, would hardly need telling if our imaginations were not so enfeebled by their lazy dependence on the ready-mades and

reach-me-downs of the ragshop in which Romance keeps its stock of 'happy endings' to misfit all stories . . . people in all directions have assumed, for no other reason than that she became the heroine of a romance, that she must have married the hero of it. This is unbearable, not only because her little drama, if acted on such a thoughtless assumption, must be spoiled, but because the true sequel is patent to anyone with a sense of human nature in general, and of feminine nature in particular.

Shaw continues for several pages and the upshot is that Eliza marries – Freddy. Probably. Almost certainly, given that (Shaw says) she had the choice between a lifetime of fetching Higgins's slippers and a lifetime of Freddy fetching hers.

The convention is that a comedy or a romance ends in/with marriage. When you put it like that it sounds a bit brutal, but that is the way Shaw, Fauchois and Renoir do put it. If the comedy and romance are to go on, there must *not* be a marriage. But this line of argument has assumed that we are dealing with comedies as belonging to some clearly defined category as recognised by Aristotle.

I don't think this is the case. The genre of *Boudu* is mixed, as hard to fit into a conventional category as a Shakespeare play. The plot of *Romeo and Juliet* leads us to call it a tragedy, but its mood and poetry are those of comedies such as *As You Like It* and *A Midsummer Night's Dream*. On the other hand *Measure for Measure* is usually listed as a comedy, but its dark mood reminds us of the tragedies. Indeed Dr Johnson was so terrified by Claudio's speech contemplating death that he could barely read it: 'Ay, but to die, and go we know not where; to lie in cold obstruction and to rot.' The plays written between *Hamlet* and *Othello* (that is to say, *Measure for Measure*, *All's Well* and *Troilus and Cressida*) have been called the 'dark comedies' or 'problem plays'. In that sense *Boudu* is a problem film.

6
. . . .

The editors of the Oxford Shakespeare say of *Measure for Measure* that 'Each of the "good" characters fails in some respect; none of the "bad" ones lacks some redeeming quality; all are, in the last analysis, "desperately mortal".' This sounds very much like the world of Renoir's films. There are no irredeemably bad characters, nor are there 'good' characters who do not have human weaknesses.

La Chienne starts with the Guignol. The characters are introduced one by one and then the commentary says that this is not a comedy or a tragedy. Renoir called its style '*drame gai*' which mixes farce and tragedy. Guignol himself introduces the story by saying that what we are about to see is neither a drama nor a comedy. It has no moral intentions and will prove nothing to you. The characters are neither heroes nor villains. They are just poor human beings like you and me.

....

Who but Shakespeare could have thrown off a phrase such as 'desperately mortal'? The words are put into the mouth of the Provost in *Measure for Measure* to describe Barnadine, who the dramatis personae calls 'a dissolute condemned prisoner'. The plot of the play is of operatic complexity: Barnardine is introduced for one specific reason. He is on what would now be called Death Row. So is Claudio, 'a young gentleman'. The idea is that to save Claudio's life the execution should be carried out on Barnardine and that the severed head should be passed off as that of Claudio. Whatever the morality of this ruse there is no doubt as to what Barnardine's function is. He has been brought into the play for the sole purpose of having his head cut off.

Now comes one of the most extraordinary moments in Shakespeare's works. Shakespeare was not capable of failing to give his characters life, and accordingly before he bumps off Barnardine he has to bring him alive. The Provost of the prison describes Barnardine as 'a Bohemian born, but here nursed up and bred; one that is a prisoner nine years old . . . A man that apprehends death no more fearfully but as a drunken sleep; careless, reckless, and fearless of what's past, present or to come; insensible of mortality, and desperately mortal.' The Provost says that Barnardine has always had 'the liberty of the prison' but 'Give him leave to escape hence, he would not. Drunk many times a day, if not many days entirely drunk. We have very oft awaked him as if to carry him to execution, and showed him a seeming warrant for it; it hath not moved him at all.'

Clearly Barnardine is a blood brother of Boudu. Where matters of life and death are concerned he is simply indifferent. When they try to execute him, Barnardine tells them to go away because he wants to sleep. He is, the Duke says, 'unfit to live or die'. It seems as though Shakespeare simply doesn't have the heart to kill Barnardine. A new ruse has to be devised to save the life of Claudio, and at the end of the play the Duke tells Barnardine:

> Sirrah, thou art said to have a stubborn soul
> That apprehends no further than this world,
> And squar'st thy life according.

And then pardons him.

The gallows humour of *Measure for Measure* seems to me related to the suicide humour of *Boudu*. Just as Barnardine and Boudu are both indifferent to death they are both, as the Duke says, stubborn souls that apprehend no further than this world and square their lives according.

At this point we begin to see the confluence of the Shakespeare–Shaw–Fauchois–Simon–Renoir streams. Michel Simon's career started with *Measure for Measure*. He also played in Shaw's *Androcles and the Lion* (as Caesar, though he would have made a splendid Androcles, or – come to think of it – the lion) and also in Shaw's *Candida* as Burgess ('a vulgar ignorant guzzling man'). These were productions by Georges Pitoëff, whose wife Ludmilla was the first French Saint Joan (Théâtre des Arts, 28 April 1925). The Pitoëffs also did Shaw's *The Apple Cart* and *Caesar and Cleopatra*. A scenario of *Pygmalion* was written by Albert Rièra, assistant director to Vigo on *Zéro de Conduite* and *L'Atalante*, but unfortunately was never produced.

Back to Shakespeare, whom Simon admired enormously. 'Everything is in Shakespeare,' he said. His favourite line was Macbeth's about life being 'A tale told by an idiot, Full of sound and fury, signifying nothing'. He wanted to act Hamlet, and there was an unrealised project for a Simon–Renoir film of the play. It would certainly have been unlike any other *Hamlet* or Hamlet, because Simon could do anything. What a Falstaff he would have been; what a Lear!

It was *Measure for Measure* that launched Simon's stage success. What is remarkable is that the part he played, the Justice, has only three lines, and they are hardly Shakespeare's most memorable:

> ESCALUS: What o'clock, think you?
> JUSTICE: Eleven, sir.
> ESCALUS: I pray you home to dinner with me.
> JUSTICE: I humbly thank you.
> ESCALUS: It grieves me for the death of Claudio. But there's no remedy.
> JUSTICE: Lord Angelo is severe.

Not a lot to work on, but apparently Simon hammed it up to such an extent that he spun out the exchange for ten minutes of grimaces, dragging his feet, losing his way, gesticulating. It's the kind of thing that infuriates producers and other actors, but audiences often love it. Evidently they did on this occasion.

In the 1920s and 1930s Simon played not only in Shaw but also in Pirandello, Ibsen, Chekhov and Gorky. As a sedimentologist and source-searcher I was particularly pleased to find that he played Eliza's Boudu-like father Doolittle in *Pygmalion* in 1925 and 1926. In *Hamlet* he played the gravedigger, doubling the role with Polonius's servant Reynaldo. He was also in another production of *Measure for Measure* where he had the wonderfully comic part of Elbow. This is much bigger than that of the Justice, but still enabled him to double with another part – yes, Barnardine.

Michel Simon was born in 1895, the year after Renoir, the same year as Jean Giono and Marcel Pagnol, and the same year as the one in which the Lumière brothers showed off their entertaining invention. Simon's birthplace was Geneva, which in some perverse way may explain his hatred of Rousseau (also a Genevan) and Voltaire (who chose the Geneva area for his exile).

Simon was conscripted into the Swiss army in 1914, but was soon out of uniform through a combination of insubordination and tuberculosis. He was variously a boxer, a boxing instructor, a right-wing anarchist, a frequenter of prostitutes, pimps and petty crooks. He was extremely well-read, a great lover of animals (especially monkeys), a talented photographer, a hypochondriac, a misanthrope (he especially hated actors), a handyman with considerable mechanical skills, owner of a vast collection of pornography and with a reputation for unorthodox sexual behaviour which he did not bother to deny.

Whether or not he was a pleasant man, he was certainly a complex one, with a good deal of Boudu in him. Renoir called him 'a genius of an actor', one so versatile that he compared him with such Renaissance figures as Leonardo and Benvenuto Cellini. He said that '*Boudu* was conceived primarily to make use of the genius of Michel Simon'.

Simon's acting career started in Geneva in 1920 with the Pitoëffs. In that year he appeared in *Measure for Measure*, *Hamlet* and Gorky's *The Lower Depths*. In the next two years he appeared in productions of (among others) Chekhov's *The Seagull*, Oscar Wilde's *Salome* and Shaw's *Androcles and the Lion*. In 1923 he moved to Paris where he appeared in no fewer than ten plays, which included *Measure for Measure* again and Shaw's *Candida* and *Pygmalion*. So it was an actor on the crest of the wave who in 1925 appeared on stage as Boudu. He was in a position to pick and choose. Clearly Michel Simon had a higher regard for Fauchois' play than has been accorded to it by writers on Renoir. Perhaps this is why Simon had such reservations about Renoir's change of ending. Even so, Simon said that *Boudu* was his favourite film.

> It was the only time in my career that someone gave me money and allowed me to be the producer. I immediately hired Jean Renoir to direct me. We were not restricted by the commercial aspects of cinema. And the results were far beyond our expectations. The audience *hated* the film. They screamed and flew into an immediate rage. When they began tearing the seats apart, the police were called and *Boudu* closed after three days.

The extent to which Simon got into a role took an extreme form in the making of *La Chienne*, where life imitated art all too closely. In the film Simon falls in love with Janie Marèze, and he did so off-screen as well, while Janie Marèze fell for Georges Flamant, who plays the pimp. After the film had been finished Flamant, who could hardly drive, took Marèze for a drive, crashed the car and she was killed. At the funeral a heart-broken Simon fainted and had to be supported as he walked past the grave. Renoir says, 'I have encountered many actors who lived their parts, but none of them followed Pirandello to this extent. Michel Simon was no longer himself, he *was* Maurice Legrand.' What Renoir doesn't mention is that he and producer Pierre Braunberger had encouraged the relationship between Flamant and Marèze in order to get the utmost conviction into their performances (Flamant was a professional criminal but an amateur actor), and at the funeral a distraught Simon threatened Renoir with a gun, saying that the death of Maréze was all his fault. 'Kill me if you like,' responded Renoir, 'but I have made the film.'

In the history of cinema there have been few actors of such greatness as that of Michel Simon. His range was enormous. He could delight or disgust, and in *Boudu* he does both. He could command your laughter or your tears with equal economy. He didn't just interpret a part or give a performance of what had been conceived and written by someone else; he was a major dramatic artist in his own right.

It is the confluence of Shakespeare, Shaw, Fauchois, Renoir and Simon that make *Boudu sauvé des eaux* the great river it is.

7

Shakespeare's plays are full of characters who are saved from the water, from Viola and Sebastian in *Twelfth Night* to Perdita in *The Winter's Tale*. In *The Tempest* all the characters are in one way or another *sauvés des eaux* – all except Ariel, who belongs to the air, and Caliban who is of the earth earthy, and is a native of the island. The magician Prospero is a bit like Lestingois, controlling everyone through the power of his books. He is an intellectual and a dreamer of dreams while Caliban is like Boudu, half-animal. Caliban is not stupid, though, and in these post-colonial times it is hard not to sympathise with him against Prospero who, as Caliban rightly says, robbed him of his isle. Our sympathies nowadays go to the victim rather than the oppressor, to the slave Caliban rather than the slave-owning Prospero.

Caliban is (like Barnardine, like Shylock, like Malvolio, perhaps even like Richard III, Iago and Macbeth) someone the plot requires us to dislike. Perhaps Shakespeare's contemporary audience did dislike them; we, on the whole, don't. One reason is that Shakespeare's view of humanity was such that he simply could not fail to empathise with his characters, and even if *tout comprendre* is not *tout pardonner* it is a big step in that direction.

Renoir is similar. He is reluctant to condemn a character. He was an *ancien combattant*, indeed a *mutilé de guerre*, whose war wound caused his limp; it gave him constant pain, and required dressing to the end of his life. This didn't make Renoir at all anti-German (or, one must add, pro-German). He said of *La Grande illusion* that he just couldn't take sides. The film ends with the Germans *not* shooting the escaped French prisoners. Renoir said of the film: 'My chief aim was the one which I have been pursuing ever since I started making films – to express the common humanity of man.' He was fond of quoting the words in Kipling's *Jungle Book* where Mowgli addresses the cobras: 'We're of the same blood, you and I.'

If this applies to cobras, does it apply to Nazis as well? The answer has to be affirmative; any other answer would be to subscribe to the Nazis' own idea of *Untermenschen*. Still, it would be (and indeed is) a severe test for someone of Renoir's sensibilities. Perhaps this is partly why he spent the Second World War in the United States. He made *La vie est à nous*, which was sponsored by the Communist Party, as part of the anti-Nazi struggle; *La Grande illusion* was banned in Italy by Mussolini, Goebbels called it 'Cinematographic Enemy Number One', and during the occupation all prints were confiscated. Even so, it is not possible to imagine Renoir making a film such as Rossellini's *Rome, Open City*. In Renoir's world, as in his father's paintings, hard edges are softened and everything is given a little glow which at best is like a glimpse of Paradise, and at worst is sentimental.

Nowadays we tend to identify with, or empathise with, the outsider: the Jew Shylock, the cracked Malvolio, the slave Caliban, the hunchback Richard III. And it is these characters – like Milton's Satan, again like Macbeth and Iago – who are the ones that have all the energy. Caliban makes everyone else in the play look effete. And, of course, all of these are smashing parts for the actors.

That is true of Boudu, but then when Michel Simon came along any part was a smashing one. Charles Granval (then husband of Madeleine Renaud) gives a wonderfully sensitive and sympathetic performance as Lestingois, but it is lightweight compared with Simon's.

But this is Renoir's work as well as Simon's. Like Shakespeare, Renoir cannot hold back sympathy. The pimp in *La Chienne* is a thoroughly nasty piece of work, but what swagger he has, what *style*. Even the brutal Uncle Jeff in *La Fille de l'eau* has (like Caliban) an energy that makes everyone else look a bit feeble, and in the final scene (when Uncle Jeff has been thrown in the river) he drifts away shaking his fist. Horrible as he is, Jeff's defiance is in its way magnificent, like Macbeth's, Iago's or Richard III's. Among Milton's finest lines are the ones about the unconquerable will, and the courage never to submit or yield. They are given to the Arch-Enemy, Satan.

This Shakespearean even-handedness in Renoir is never clearer than in *Boudu*. Lestingois is in most respects highly admirable. He is intelligent and he is kind. There is poetry in his soul, he is humorous. His touchstones are the enlightened and humanist ones of Voltaire (Houdon's bust of Voltaire is one of the first things we see in the bookshop) and Anatole France (a regular customer at the shop, we are told). Lestingois is lacking in such common vices as the need for power or greed for money. He is extremely generous: he gives valuable books to the impoverished poetry-loving student. He not only pours out money on Boudu but also gives him the winning lottery ticket (in the play Boudu gets the ticket by deceit, swapping it with his own losing ticket; when Boudu admits to this, Lestingois is so impressed by his honest confession of dishonesty that he forgives him).

What is more, Lestingois has considerable physical courage. Of the hundreds who swarm to see the drowning man in the river it is this tubby little middle-aged sedentary bibliophile who is the man of action and decision, the one who actually throws himself into the water and saves a man's life.

One of his neighbours exclaims admiringly that it should be a member of *our* class (*notre rang*) who risked his life like this. Lestingois wouldn't have said that: he isn't at all class-conscious. He doesn't hesitate to take the disgusting tramp into his house; it is not Lestingois but his wife who objects to this physically disruptive cuckoo who takes over their tidy nest, shattering domestic order in every sense. Whatever we may think about Lestingois he would never say, as Prospero does of Caliban, 'I have used thee, Filth as thou art, with human care, and lodged thee In mine own cell.' Lestingois is far too polite to call someone filth, and he is altogether more admirable than Prospero, who is a bully and a tyrant, and a poseur and a bit of a bore. Lestingois is in fact a person of exceptional quality. In his way he is as much *hors série*, as much a one-off, as Boudu.

But Renoir does not make the mistake of showing Lestingois as *un chevalier sans peur et sans reproche*. His treatment of the women in the film is not at all correct. In his different way he is as egotistic as Boudu. With all his altruism his main concern is (like that of most of us) his own comfort. Whereas Boudu's world is one of physically uncomfortable freedom, Lestingois' is by contrast a prison, however comfortable and 'civilised'.

I referred to Boudu as a disgusting tramp. Boudu *is* disgusting. In the safety of our cinema seats we may find him funny, we may even identify with him, but he is still disgusting. Few of us would show the tolerance of Lestingois. We would have him out of the house as soon as feasibly and humanely possible. I also called him a tramp, which I think is the right word in English. In French it is *clochard*. In American English tramp means a prostitute or promiscuous woman, so hobo or bum is probably the right word on that side of the Atlantic. In practice, writers in English repeatedly refer to Boudu as a hippy.

Boudu didn't reach the United States until 1967. The *New York Times* called it 'a second-rate antique', the *New York Post* said 'It is easily dismissed' and *World Journal Tribune* said it didn't need rescuing. On the West Coast, by contrast, it had a splendid reception. Alexander Sesonske says that the '*Los Angeles Free Press* considered its Los Angeles premiere a major event and quickly identified Boudu as the first hippy, born thirty years too soon.' Pauline Kael hailed the film as 'not only a lovely fable about a bourgeois attempt to reform an early hippy . . . but a photographic record of an earlier France'.

In the same year François Truffaut in his introduction to a Renoir festival said: 'All the words that evoke laughter can be used about Boudu: droll, buffoon, burlesque, incongruous. The theme of *Boudu* is vagabondage, the temptation to try to pass from one class to another, the importance of the natural; Boudu was a hippy long before the word was invented.' Penelope Gilliatt called Boudu 'the haywire tramp whose way of life anticipates the hippies by nearly forty years'. Renoir himself said (*My Life and My Films*, 1974) that 'Boudu foreshadowed the hippy movement long before it came into being – indeed he was the perfect hippy.'

The Oxford English Dictionary says that hippie or hippy is a hipster; a person usually exotically dressed, who is, or is taken to be, given to the use of hallucinogenic drugs; a beatnik. In the Collins Dictionary a hippy or hippie is (especially during the 1960s) a person whose behaviour, dress, use of drugs etc. implies a rejection of conventional values. Hip is a slang word meaning aware of or following the latest trends in music, ideas, fashion, etc.

None of this sounds remotely like Boudu. Boudu is certainly not exotically dressed. If he thought the children would laugh at him if he wore a frock-coat in the street, what chance would there be of getting him to wear psychedelic colours with flared trousers? He does not take drugs. When he first tastes wine he spits it out, and even when he is most house-trained there is no suggestion that he is other than a moderate drinker. After all, water is his element – earth and water, that's Boudu. He does smoke a cigar at the height of his besuited embourgeoisement, but he only puffs at it, and I think we can say that, like President Clinton, he didn't inhale.

We are told the hippies rejected conventional values. Boudu doesn't reject conventional values: he never had them in the first place. Michel Simon called Boudu a *pique-assiette*, which means something like a sponger or parasite, and he said that what he had learnt from Boudu was that one attitude to take to society is to loathe it (*'c'est de la vomir'*). Boudu may spew society out of his mouth: you wouldn't catch him doing anything as pussy-footing as 'rejecting conventional values'.

It is a comic idea just to imagine the words 'rejecting conventional values' being said by Boudu. Words have a different meaning when Boudu uses them. After Boudu has behaved particularly badly, Lestingois tells him, *'Faudra changer de conduite, mon ami'* ('You're going to have to change your behaviour, my friend'). To which Boudu replies by merely repeating the words in a mocking tone: *'Fau-dra chan-ger de con-duite, mon a-mi.'* It's a rather brilliant reply, showing for one thing that the chances of his changing his behaviour are nil.

Apart from beards and long hair there is (as far as I can see) nothing in common between Boudu and the hippies. Their drop-outs mostly dropped in again and are now in well-heeled jobs. Boudu was just the opposite: he was a temporary drop-in. Of course one can see why *Boudu* should have had a special appeal on the West Coast in 1967. A work as rich as this can be interpreted in many ways and in the late 1960s it seemed appropriate to see Boudu as a proto-hippy or *soixante-huitard* (one of the generation of the May 1968 events). Boudu was not remotely like the middle-class students of France, Italy, Britain and the United States who briefly caused their governments some local difficulties. Boudu isn't middle-class, and he is equally not working-class – he positively rejects the idea of work (a point made by the factory whistle at the end, heard while Boudu rolls on the ground in the freedom of the other side of the river). Boudu is classless. He is outside the class system. He is what the French call a *marginal*.

The last statement goes against the grain of the interpretation that succeeded that of Boudu the Hippy. This was even more improbable: Boudu the Working-Class Hero. It's already hard to remember the way of thinking before the Wall came down, when Marx meant Karl rather than Groucho. If anyone wants reminding I refer them to Christopher Faulkner's *The Social Cinema of Jean Renoir* (Princeton University Press, 1986), which is much concerned with the class struggle and discusses *Boudu* in this light. Faulkner is surely mistaken. If anything *Boudu* the film is anarchist, though Boudu himself (who is very much Michel Simon) is not so much anarchist as anarchic. The distinction I am making is between anarchy and chaos. Bakunin, Kropotkin and Tolstoy were anarchists. Boudu is chaotic.

8
....

I have written elsewhere[5] about the relationship between fools, clowns, tricksters, prophets, the man on the donkey and Holy Fools. I'm not clear what is Boudu's precise relationship to all these, but he is more a Fool, a clown or a trickster than he is a hippy or a working-class hero. Mostly, I think, he's a fool.

In Ben Jonson's *Volpone* there is a song about fools:

They are the only nation
Worth men's envy or admiration;

> Free from care or sorrow-taking,
> Selves and others merry-making . . .
> O, who would not be
> He, he, he?

Clown, trickster, joker, buffoon, jester, fool – in various forms this strange figure, laughing or laughed at, exists both outside the norms of society and at the same time somewhere very near the centre of human experience. He is an amalgam of gluttony, stupidity, sexuality, cunning, shiftlessness, malice, deceit and truth-telling. He breaks down distinctions between wisdom and folly, sanity and insanity, rule and disorder. He makes us laugh and he is often (like Socrates and Jesus) the scapegoat.

In the pack of cards there are fifty-two plus the Joker. The Joker has no suit and belongs to no family, but because he can change shape, because he is 'wild', he is more powerful than the King or the Ace. While the King is sovereign, the Joker is nothing and everything. As against the King's law he is lawlessness, and between the two of them the King and the Fool rule the court.

This pair, Master and Fool, crops up throughout history, mythology and literature. Lear and the Fool, Hal and Falstaff, Pantagruel and Panurge, Don Quixote and Sancho Panza, Pickwick and Sam Weller, Holmes and Watson, there are endless and subtle variations on the theme. Wooster and Jeeves are a neat reversal of the Master–Fool relationship. Usually it is the straight man who is the protagonist, as Lestingois is in Fauchois' play (even if it is Boudu whose name is in the title). In the film the two are on fairly equal terms in the middle (that is to say, the Fauchois part). In the beginning and at the end, and in the film as a whole, there is no doubt that it is the Fool, Boudu, who is the Hero.

The Fool is a Trickster, he is Hermes, he is Harpo, he is pure Libido, wilfully destructive, uncontrollably sexual and with an appetite that (in Harpo's case) enables him to eat buttons, telephones, ties and cigars with relish. 'He's half goat,' Chico explains. So is Boudu, who almost the last time we see him is sharing a meal with a goat, just as when we first saw him he was eating with a dog. Boudu is more than once referred to as an animal, sometimes as a pig. He rolls about on the dining-room table, can't get used to sleeping in a bed, swings from the door lintel in simian fashion, goes on all fours, eats with his fingers, can barely speak, and altogether suggests that he belongs to some earlier stage of evolution than the rest of us. (Harpo sleeps with a horse in *Duck Soup*, has a pet frog in *Monkey Business*, and the chorus of black kids in *At the Circus* sing the words 'That man don't belong to the human race'.) Harpo's fright wig is similar to Boudu's hairstyle. It seems highly likely that Renoir and Simon would have seen the early Marx Brothers films. Antonin Artaud, writing about the Marx Brothers in the 1930s, said that 'if there is a characteristic state, a distinct poetic degree of the spirit that can be called Surrealism, *Animal Crackers* shares that entirely.' (*Animal Crackers* was made in 1930, *Boudu* in 1932.)

These agents of chaos who upset the ordered respectable standards of the waking world are laughable because they act out our secret desires. If *we* see a big bum we might want to kick it: Chaplin *does* kick it. The great clowns from Max Linder, Keaton and Chaplin to

Harpo in Horse Feathers

Laurel and Hardy, the Marx Brothers, Boudu and Hulot are the enemies of conformity, of what can be regulated. They are the awkward squad. Any civilization needs orderly people like Lestingois, but humanity also needs the quirky, individual, eccentric, unpredictable, chaotic and undisciplined. We need the checks and balances of order and disorder; we need both Lestingois and Boudu.

In the 1960s there was a debate between Kenneth Tynan and Eugène Ionesco after Tynan had criticised Ionesco for his lack of commitment and social engagement. Ionesco wrote:

> I also think it possible for man not to be a social animal. A child has great difficulty in fitting into society, he struggles against it and finds it hard to adapt himself to it. . . . And if a child finds it hard to adapt himself to society, it is because there is in human nature something that has to escape the social order or be alienated by it.

That's Boudu.

9

In something as complex as *Boudu*, the themes, direction, acting, narrative, dialogue and everything else are too closely connected with one another for it always to be possible to discuss one at a time. Some degree of overlapping and repetition is inevitable. In one way or another the preceding pages have referred to most parts of the film, though not always in the order in which things happen on the screen. In fact the pack has been thoroughly shuffled. What follows is an attempt at a more orderly account, from beginning to end, partly in note form, especially when skimming over scenes and themes that have already been discussed in some detail.

The first image, behind the credits, is of light playing on gently rippling water, while strings play the melody of 'Sur les bords de la Riviera'. Then, to the sound of a flute, we see a small stage onto which skips a nymph pursued by a vine-covered Pan. A rather portly Pan. In a dramatic gesture he leans against a classical column which, being made of cardboard, nearly falls over. All pastoral is artificial; this pastoral is amateur as well.

The next scene is the bookseller's shop, with its shelves of old volumes and Houdon's bust of Voltaire. The nymph, now in modern dress (polka-dot blouse), is the housemaid Anne-Marie (Séverine Lerczinska). The portly Pan who is embracing her is the bookseller Edouard Lestingois (Charles Granval), smartly dressed with a watch-chain across his embonpoint, stroking and fondling the charming if slightly plain young girl while shooting a pastoral line of love-talk about nuptials and Priapus: '. . . *et, toute nue, les nuits d'été, danser au clair de lune. Bacchus eût présidé le festin nuptial de Priape Lestingois . . . et de Chloé Anne-Marie!*' Nude dancing by moonlight on summer nights . . . Bacchus presiding over the nuptial banquet of Priapus Lestingois and Chloé Anne-Marie. He complains that his excellent wife is completely unable to make him feel the innocent joys of the flesh any more.

Lestingois with the house-maid

'*Je vous aime, Monsieur Lestingois,*' says Anne-Marie. (By contrast Boudu immediately addresses Madame Lestingois with the familiar *tu*.) Lestingois sends Anne-Marie off to the kitchen to make the soup, and tells her not to forget the salt. She replies flirtatiously that she won't forget 'while thinking about . . . tonight'. Lestingois sighs. 'She is charming,' he says, 'but I'm growing old . . . my pipes are tired (*mes pipeaux sont fatigués*) . . . and soon some shepherd will take her off me, with his new flute.' He seems resigned to the prospect but not desolated.

Exterior of a Paris Left Bank bookshop that could come from an Atget or Lartigue photograph. Madame Lestingois enters the shop looking bored and petulant.

Already three themes have been introduced: water; the pastoral in an urban setting; and the Feydeau-like domestic triangle of husband, disaffected wife and young housemaid-mistress.

Boudu with his dog

Change of scene to water. A fine-looking yacht is in full sail. This turns out to be a toy boat on a pond in a park, with a struggle going on between a woman and her charge, the young boy toy-yachtsman.

Now for the first time we see Boudu, sitting at the bottom of a tree with a dog. He looks *like* the Michel Simon tramp at the end of *La Chienne* but is not the same: no more than Heraclitus with rivers could Simon step into the same part twice. He was shaggy at the end of *La Chienne*. He's shaggier now. He is growling as much as singing 'Sur les bords de la Riviera, On murmure une brise embaumée' (the words are hard to make out). Renoir explains somewhere that this was a popular nightclub song of the time, so that it is as if Boudu is singing 'The Man Who Broke the Bank at Monte Carlo'. The strange thing (if you are familiar with the words of that song) is that while Boudu is clearly not a millionaire, and he does not walk with an independent air, he *is* in the Bois de Boulogne.

Black, the dog, is black and definitely *un chien*, not *une chienne*. Boudu isn't really stroking Black. It's more as though he is searching him for vermin. The two of them are like chimps grooming one another. It is common for dog and owner to come to resemble one another, and Black and Boudu are a good example. They are both very hairy.

The woman and the boy carrying his toy yacht pass by, see Boudu and Black and hurry away in alarm. Boudu pushes the dog away. He later describes Black as *frisoté*, frizzy or, as one might say in English, shaggy. Black is a shaggy dog. Is this a shaggy dog story?

The dog goes to the edge of the pond and there's a shot which lasts a long time in which Black (as is often the way with great actors) simply does nothing. Suddenly he sees something (another dog, we suppose) and runs out of frame, never to be seen again.

Back to Boudu at the foot of the tree chewing bread, singing 'Sur les bords de la Riviera' in his strangled, guttural voice. He calls for Black. He gets up and shambles round the park, asking if anyone has seen a shaggy dog. He meets a man (Jacques Becker, better known as a film director than as an actor); he is sitting on a park bench, either drunk or mad, and answers Boudu by getting to his feet and making strange wordless noises and inarticulate gestures. There is no explanation, and the man does not appear in the film again.

Now comes a shot with Renoir's signature all over it. It is in deep focus and for about a minute and a quarter the camera doesn't move, framing the action as statically as the proscenium arch of a theatre. Against the background of the park's flat surface and trees, people come and go as on a stage, either from one side of the screen to the other, or straight towards or away from the camera. They avoid Boudu. He asks the park guard if he has seen a shaggy dog and is told to go away. A young blonde woman in an enormous hat asks the guard if he has seen *her* lost dog, a Pekinese which is worth 10,000 francs. She is treated with great attention. Evidently the way the owners of lost dogs are treated depends on their class, wealth and sex.

A large open car stops and the rather flabby driver offers the woman his help in looking for the valuable dog. She gets in and they drive off. To look for the dog or to spend their time in some other way?

Boudu is lying on a bench when a woman and child pass. 'Give

this to the poor man,' the woman says to the child. 'You should always
be kind to the unfortunate.' The child gives some money to Boudu, who
says, 'Why are you giving me 100 sous?' 'To buy bread,' the little girl
says.

An open car pulls up, driven by a very smart young man. Boudu
shuffles over and opens the car door. The smart young man lights a
cigarette and fumbles in his pocket in search of a tip. After a while
Boudu takes the money he has just been given by the child and gives it
to the rich man, who is astounded. 'Are you mad?' he asks. 'Are you
making fun of me?' ('*Vous . . . vous fichez de moi?*') Boudu growls, 'To buy
some bread', and shuffles off.

The poor man giving to the rich one is just the first of Boudu's
reversals of normal behaviour. It is common for the clown and the
mythological Trickster to do things the wrong way round; theirs is a
world upside down – or at least they make it one. Thus Chaplin plays

Boudu gives the rich man a tip

his violin resting on the wrong shoulder, as does Harpo with his harp, and Simon as the painter Legrand holds his artist's palette the wrong way round.

Trickster characters occur in legend (Till Eulenspiegel, for example), mythology (Hermes), and in those societies in which their role has been institutionalised as fools or jesters. There's a good example in Thomas Berger's novel *Little Big Man* where Jack Crabb's Cheyenne friend Younger Bear becomes a Contrary. He deliberately walks through sagebushes and cactus instead of avoiding them. He doesn't wash with water but with earth, and he greets Jack with a goodbye.

> Then, the way a person who has just took a bath will sit upon the bank to dry, he goes into the creek and sets down in the water. I guess it made sense, seeing how he had just washed with dirt. I realized he was doing everything backwards . . .

Younger Bear has become a Contrary . . .

> He sleeps on the bare ground, preferably an uncomfortable bit of terrain and never on a bed. He cannot marry. He lives off by himself some distance from camp.

Boudu is evidently akin to a Contrary.

The pace of the film feels unhurried, even leisurely, but simply listing the events in the short opening sequence in the park makes one realise how packed it is with incident. Though each incident is given plenty of time, one thing happens after another at almost the rate of a Tom and Jerry cartoon. And while there is constant action, at the same time points are being made and themes set out.

The use of dialogue has been very economical, and the narrative could almost be silent cinema at its best. That said, Renoir's use of sound is brilliant. There's the neighbour's flute-playing that separates the scenes, and also comments on them; there's the Boudu song 'Sur les bords de la Riviera' (which in the course of the film is sung by different people in different ways, and often without the words on instruments varying from guitar to harmonica); and the Anne-Marie song ('Les fleurs du jardin'). When we hear Boudu humming Anne-Marie's song, or Lestingois humming Boudu's, we don't need to be told in words what they are thinking about.

And there are the factory noises, the crunch of gravel, the street sounds of traffic, and the barrel-organ and the triumphant trumpets, trombone and drums of the parade which comes to announce that Lestingois is to be decorated for his bravery. Had Renoir done nothing else to Fauchois' play, his use of sound would have transformed it.

The Anne-Marie song:

Les fleurs du jardin
Chaque soir ont du chagrin
Oui, mais dès l'aurore
Tous leurs chagrins s'évaporent
Quel est l'enchanteur
Quel guérit tant de douleurs,
Quel est ce ma-gi-ci-en?
C'est le soleil.

L'hiver dans les bois
Les oiseaux meurent de froid.
Leurs nuits dans les branches
Sont comme des tombes blanches.
Avril reparaît
Et soudain dans la forêt
Mille voix en même temps
Bénissent le printemps.

Mon printemps est mon sourire
Quand mon coeur souffle et soupire
Ton sourire est mon printemps
Mon printemps . . .

I said Boudu shuffles off, but shuffles isn't the right word. Shambles? No, there's no right word for Boudu's walk. There are actors whose walk is as expressive as their faces. Hulot's walk is the best thing Jacques Tati ever did. The pride and excitement of James Dean's walk in *Giant* as he paces out the land which he has just acquired. Or the way

Gary Cooper walks in *High Noon*: with a walk like that you don't need to say much more than 'Yep' and 'Nope'. Alec Guinness has a whole range of walks not only in *Kind Hearts and Coronets* where he plays several roles, but also in his one part in *The Man in the White Suit*. It's the same in this film. Here the shambling shuffle of the hunched figure tells us that it is not bread or money that this 'unfortunate' needs. We are looking at someone in his own lower depths, someone who might easily just throw himself in the river, and nobody would care, not even a dog.

Scene: the bookshop. The student (Jean Dasté, the teacher in *Zéro de Conduite*, Jean in *L'Atalante*) is told that the price of a book, *Les Lettres d'Hamabed*, is 50 francs, which is more than he can afford (the dog the woman lost in the park was worth two hundred times as much).

> LESTINGOIS: You like Voltaire? You are right.
> STUDENT: It's him who's right.

Lestingois is imbued with the spirit of Voltaire and of Anatole France, a regular customer at the shop. (The *quais* near the Pont des Arts have changed hardly at all in the more than half a century since the film was made. There are still antique bookshops just like that of Lestingois, with wrought-iron window balconies on the upper storeys. Appropriately the *quais* here are today named after Voltaire and Anatole France.)

Not only does Lestingois give the book to the young man, but also gives him another book for good measure. Fifty francs may mean less to Lestingois than 100 sous to Boudu, but evidently both of them are generous. The young man is as surprised at Lestingois' gift as the rich man was at Boudu's.

> STUDENT: But you don't know me.
> LESTINGOIS: I know you; you are called Youth.

A neat example of Lestingois' sentimentality, his tendency to turn things and people into romantic abstractions, and also of his trust, good nature and generosity. If Boudu embodies nature, Lestingois embodies good nature.

We don't know the end of this story. My guess is that the student first read the books and then sold them. That way everyone is happy. The student has read Voltaire and got some francs, and Lestingois has the pleasure of thinking what a generous man and Lover of Youth he is. Or did the student read the books and return them, or did he come back years later and pay for them? The fact that we can speculate in this way shows how even a very small role in a Renoir film carries the suggestion of a life going on outside the drama (as with Shakespeare: Bradley's notorious question was, How many children had Lady Macbeth?)

A tug-boat on the Seine. Lots of black smoke and steam as in Monet's picture of the Gare St Lazare. Boudu is walking along the *quai* past the *bouquinistes* (the open-air bookstalls selling second-hand books). Boudu is seen from above from the window of Lestingois' drawing-room. Boudu is scratching the back of his neck. Vans and cars

You like Voltaire...
and with good reason

Lestingois with the student

pass between him and the camera which follows him walking along the pavement in a 40-second shot.

Interior: Anne-Marie singing her song. She is polishing a telescope which she rubs up and down with an expression that suggests that her thoughts are elsewhere. She looks through the wrong end of the telescope. Lestingois comes in and takes the telescope. Anne-Marie starts cleaning the piano.

ANNE-MARIE: Why do you have a piano when no one plays it?
LESTINGOIS: Because we are respectable people.

This exchange (which is in the Fauchois play as well) is the kind of thing that leads some people to see the film as being about class and as showing the totally bourgeois nature of Lestingois, which means that he is a bad egg. One critic after another has parroted a version of the film in which Renoir (unlike Fauchois, apparently) attacks the middle class as represented by the Lestingois household. This is nonsense. Lestingois is an admirable figure and he is treated with affection. When Renoir wants to express dislike he can do it with a click of the fingers, as he does with the idle rich in the park at the beginning of the film. He does no such thing with the bookseller. The other point about Lestingois' remark about the piano is that it is a joke. He is a highly intelligent man with a keen sense of irony.

He looks out of the window through the telescope, concentrating on the ankles of the girls going by. This makes Anne-Marie jealous. She pouts and sulks. Lestingois tells her that jealousy is worthy neither of her character nor of her beauty. On hearing this flowery speech she starts dusting the equally artificial flowers and the stuffed dead birds over the respectable piano.

The interiors were shot in a studio on a set specially made to Renoir's requirements. This gives him the opportunity for the deep-focus shots for which he is celebrated. He uses doorways and windows to frame shots like an easel painting or the stage of a theatre or Punch and Judy show. Now, he frames the picture in an entirely novel way.

Lestingois catches sight of Boudu through the telescope, the picture being in a circular frame. I wonder if Hitchcock had this shot in mind in *Rear Window* when James Stewart looks from a similar viewpoint through his telephoto lens at the murderer in the garden below. Here, Boudu walks up the steps to the footbridge, while Anne-Marie continues to sing. Lestingois hushes her. 'Oooh!' he exclaims on spotting Boudu. 'I've never seen such a perfect specimen of a tramp.'

Renoir says: 'I obtained a very long lens, the kind of lens that is used in Africa to film lions from afar. But instead of filming a lion, I filmed Michel Simon. I stationed my camera in a second-floor window, so that I would be above the roofs of the cars going by, as Michel Simon walked along the embankment, through the streets of Paris, among people who didn't notice him.' This is not only long before Godard did something similar with Belmondo and Jean Seberg in *Breathless*, it's also more successful. In Godard's film passers-by turn their heads to look at the actors: they may not have spotted the camera but they knew a film was being made. No one turns to look at Boudu. It's rude to stare.

With his beard and long hair and ragged clothes Boudu looks like everyone's idea of Robinson Crusoe, but in terms of relationships it is Lestingois who is Crusoe and Boudu is the potential Friday. Crusoe/ Lestingois first sees Friday/Boudu through a telescope and then in the water. 'Here I observed, by the help of my perspective glass . . . two miserable wretches dragged from the boats . . . and . . . brought out for the slaughter.' Crusoe intervenes with his rifle and rescues the poor wretch. This is not for humanitarian reasons. Even while the chase is going on, 'It came now very warmly upon my thoughts, and indeed, irresistibly, that now was my time to get me a servant, and perhaps a companion or assistant.'

Like Lestingois, Crusoe is bookish and considers himself to be of a superior culture. Like Lestingois, he clothes Friday. He gives him 'linen drawers, a jerkin of goat's skin . . . and thus he was cloathed for the present, tolerably well, and was mighty well pleased to see himself almost as well cloathed as his master. It is true he went awkwardly in these things at first . . . but at length he took to them very well.' Just as Boudu challenges conventionally accepted notions on such subjects as where to sleep and where to spit, so Friday asks simple questions which awkwardly query some of Crusoe's basic tenets of belief. But Friday is malleable ('never man had a more faithful, loving, sincere servant') in a way in which – thank goodness – Boudu is not.

Like a scientist with his microscope, Lestingois has spotted

through his telescope a perfect specimen. Soon he will by chance acquire it and undertake the experiment of turning a *clochard* into a bookseller, as Higgins turned a flower-girl into a fair lady.

Boudu is walking across the bridge in his hunched way when he stops and with barely perceptible hesitation puts a leg over the rail. What is shocking is not so much the fact that this man has decided to end it all as the suddenness with which he acts.

This is the second sudden act in the film. The first was when Boudu's dog Black saw something interesting in the distance and suddenly ran away. A third sudden and spontaneous act of decision now follows. Lestingois downs telescope, rushes from the house, crosses the street, runs down the steps, takes off his jacket and hurls himself into the water. I have already quoted Renoir *père*'s saying that you can use the tiller to go this way or that way but you are still a cork following the current. These three actions (those of Black, Boudu and now Lestingois) are decisions that count as more than a touch on the tiller.

While Lestingois runs from the room, Anne-Marie hops up and down in excitement, gleefully exclaiming, 'Ooh, un *accident*!' Charming as she is, Anne-Marie is a bird-brain, as her reaction here confirms. In fact none of the women in the film is shown in a particularly favourable light. The women in the park are either bossing their children about or flirting or plying for trade. Madame Lestingois is a bad-tempered, sexually frustrated sour-puss, and Anne-Marie has hardly a thought in her pretty little head. None of the men is faultless either, but it would be uphill work to argue that *Boudu* is a feminist film.

So Lestingois dives into the water. Captain Mainwaring has left *Dad's Army* and is suddenly Douglas Fairbanks, but for real. Boudu is floundering in the water. On the bridge an enormous crowd has assembled to watch the exciting event. In a film full of extraordinary scenes this one is particularly odd. Such a large crowd could not have assembled so quickly after someone jumped into the river. They have not assembled to watch a man drowning but to watch a film being made, the film we are watching.

Among the crowd (in defiance of strictly possible real time) is the polka-dotted Anne-Marie, now jumping up and down with excitement at the heroism of her employer-lover. Next to her is Madame

Lestingois, so bored that she has actually turned her back on the exciting events in the water. Since she is so uninterested, why has she bothered to stir herself from her usual lethargy to leave the shop, cross the street and join the throng? And while her husband is about to become a hero or else be drowned himself, she turns her back. It doesn't make sense in realistic terms, but this is not a work of realism. In terms of the silent screen Madame Lestingois' actions are self-explanatory.

In the crowd a neighbour of Lestingois says, 'Oh, it is fine that a man of our sort should give such an example of civic courage.' Boudu is rescued, taken back to the shop, and given various alarmingly violent forms of artificial respiration by Lestingois, while Anne-Marie gazes at him with besotted admiration. So besotted that when Lestingois asks her to fetch something, the words don't get through. She goes on gazing in goofy admiration. Lestingois, concerned that Boudu will swallow his tongue, says to his wife, 'The tongue, the tongue, get the tongue out.' Whereupon she sticks out her own tongue.

As, later, does Anne-Marie

Neither of the women is of much use in this emergency, Anne-Marie being almost paralysed with admiration of Lestingois, while Madame is mostly concerned with the effect that her sopping-wet husband and his new unconscious acquisition are going to have on the upholstery. 'You're not going to bring *that* into my house,' she says.

Boudu responds with a sign of life in the form of a small fountain of water from his mouth. He speaks.

BOUDU: Am I dead?
LESTINGOIS: You're alive, you're really alive.
BOUDU: Have to start again. Going to drown. Why did you pull me out of the water?
LESTINGOIS: To save you.
BOUDU: It was to save me I threw myself in. Life disgusts me.

Boudu wanted to die and he is *never* going to be grateful for having his life saved. His attitude is that of any child. You can always say to your parent, 'I didn't ask to be born. It was your idea, not mine, so the responsibility is yours. I don't owe you anything.'

Once Boudu is on his feet Lestingois thinks about clothing him. Stripped of his rags, Boudu notices Anne-Marie and tries to paw her. The narrative continues by accumulating details and tiny incidents. Lestingois asks Boudu if he wants a tie. 'What's a tie?' Lestingois explains that it is a small piece of material you wear round your neck. Boudu can't see the point of it and Lestingois good-naturedly says that a tie is not absolutely essential (unlike a piano?). Boudu agrees to wear a frock-coat and seems quite pleased with it, but rejects the idea of wearing it in the street where the kids will laugh at him because he'll look like a *chienlit*. (This word was later made famous by President de Gaulle with reference to the May events of 1968. It may be *chien-lit* [dog-bed] or *chie-en-lit* [shit in bed]. In Boudu's case the English 'dog's breakfast' would seem appropriate.)

Lestingois is now in his dressing-gown, and Anne-Marie comes in with his bedroom slippers and bends down to put them on his feet. 'Can't he put his own slippers on?' Boudu asks. 'Why are you doing it?' 'Because I want to,' she says, and sticks her tongue out at him, which for a moment almost seems to shock Boudu.

Does he want soup? No, he doesn't want soup, and eggs give him stomach-ache. A fussy eater, Boudu. He wants *tartine* (bread and butter) and sardines. 'And hurry up,' he says to Madame Lestingois, who is putting on an air of affronted dignity worthy of Margaret Dumont in a Marx Brothers film. When the food comes Boudu eats it in a disgusting manner. According to Michel Simon it was Boudu's eating the sardines with his fingers that caused the original cinema audiences to riot, though Renoir says it was Boudu cleaning the shoe polish from his hands on the satin bed-cover which was found unacceptable.

Boudu is given a glass which, he is told, contains white wine. He drinks and immediately spits it out. He says it's sharp ('*Ça pique*'). This is not the judgment of a wine connoisseur. It is rather that, like an animal, he has an instinctive aversion to alcohol. He asks for a glass of cold water. Boudu is not a drinker. This means that the shambling, staggering, shuffling figure with slurred speech and unsteady gait we have seen so far is Boudu *sober*.

At times the way Boudu mumbles would make Marlon Brando sound like an elocution teacher. (Boudu is a part Brando would have played wonderfully.) I am reassured to find that native French-speakers also at times find Boudu's words incomprehensible, as I do with the dialogue of most American films nowadays.

Boudu eats with his fingers and cleans his shoes on the bed-cover

Madame Lestingois asks her husband what he is going to do with his new friend. Lestingois suggests a hotel, but Boudu adamantly rejects the idea. All right, they'll put a mattress on the landing.

Boudu finds in the pocket of the frock-coat a lottery ticket, which (generous as ever) Lestingois gives him. Boudu rolls on his back on the table, like a dog in a field on a sunny day. Lestingois asks what he would do if he won the 100,000 franc lottery prize. Boudu says he would buy a bicycle. Lestingois asks if he knows how to ride a bicycle. Boudu rejects the question with his usual logic. How could he know how to ride a bicycle, he asks, when he hasn't learnt?

Lestingois is smiling and laughing all the time, and now he pats and strokes an ever more doglike Boudu. At this moment the affection between Boudu and Lestingois is like that between Renoir and Godefer, or the adolescent Zola and Cézanne as described in *L'Oeuvre*. It is pure friendship, of a kind that cuts across class or any other kind of barrier. This is distilled Renoir.

Boudu asks Lestingois what he does in this big shop and Lestingois says he is a bookseller. Can Boudu read? *Grosses lettres* ('big letters'), Boudu replies with a manic laugh which makes it sound as though he has said something obscene. In Boudu's mouth anything can sound obscene.

Madame Lestingois talks to her husband about the funeral of a friend of his. Why hadn't he gone? He doesn't like funerals. Did he know his friend had a mistress? He hopes so, for his sake. While this conversation is going on Boudu seems to feel left out, and responds in a childlike manner. He diverts himself by apparently trying to do some trick with his napkin, flicking it in the air to make a knot. Instead he knocks over a glass of wine. Madame Lestingois pours salt on the tablecloth. She explains to Boudu that this is to soak up the wine (*'C'est pour pomper le vin'*). When Lestingois spills salt on the tablecloth Boudu immediately pours wine on it – to soak up the salt (*'C'est pour pomper le sel'*). It's a sort of conceptual Spoonerism. Other Contrary behaviour: at unexpected moments when it suits his mood Boudu performs handstands, which is one way of turning the world upside down.

The night scene. *Nessun dorma*. Boudu can't sleep on his mattress because it is too soft. Instead he lies on the floor at the foot of the stairs. Lestingois and Anne-Marie are in their own rooms anticipating their soon coming together. Meanwhile Madame Lestingois is alone in her bed, panting with frustrated sexual desire.

Lestingois gets out of bed with an expectant expression. Anne-Marie hears and smiles in equal expectancy. Quiet sound of *Auprès de ma blonde, il fait bon dormir*. Lestingois finds his way blocked by Boudu, who has abandoned the mattress and is using the floor as a bed and the bottom step as a pillow (compare with the Contrary in *Little Big Man*). He explains that a mattress is too soft to crash out on. And he's disgusted by the idea of sweating in sheets. Lestingois protests that the bed is a marvellous invention. 'Well, go and sleep in it,' Boudu says. One-up to Boudu.

Lestingois goes back to his room. We hear the flute again, and see Notre Dame. I'm not clear about the meaning of these recurrent images of the flute and the cathedral, which often arrive together. Is the flute that of Pan and paganism? And Notre Dame, and sometimes the nearby

Sainte-Chapelle – do they represent Christianity, or is it that (as architecture of great beauty) these buildings represent art and the works of humankind? Or all this?

It's the next day and Boudu is in great form, singing and blowing noises which sound like farts. He is wearing a suit and tie, and eats a meal without using his fingers.

We've had a small fountain of water from Boudu's mouth when he regained consciousness after nearly drowning. He has spat out the wine which he found sharp. Now he clears his throat and is about to spit when Lestingois catches him in time and expostulates. He explains that it would be disgusting to spit on the carpet: he should use a handkerchief. Boudu asks what he should then do with the handkerchief. Lestingois gestures that he should put it in his pocket. Boudu finds the idea of carrying this around with him disgusting. Boudu's contrary way of thinking scores another point. He should have invented Kleenex.

Now comes a mystery that I haven't been able to solve. In both copies of the film I have seen recently the narrative becomes confused here. There is quite a long shot of Anne-Marie in the kitchen doing not very much. I suspect that it is the kind of shot that was used in film comedy to pass the time while the audience was laughing. You can often spot them when watching a film on video on your own (especially in Marx Brothers films after Groucho has said something particularly hilarious: subsequent dialogue would be lost in the audience's laughter). My explanation is as follows. I have already mentioned that Boudu spits into the rare edition of Balzac's *La physiologie du mariage*. My recollection of seeing the film years ago is that there is a scene where Boudu goes to a bookshelf and takes out a volume. He opens it. What is he going to do? Surely he's not going to read it; he can only read big letters. No, he hawks into it, closes the book and puts it back on the shelf.

In *The Sweet Smell of Success* there is a shot of terrible violence in which the Irish cop smashes his fist into the face of the jazz musician suitor of J. J.'s sister. On seeing the film again you find that there is no such scene. What happens is a cut to Chico Hamilton's drumstick striking the side-drum. The cop's blow has been provided by your imagination. Have we similarly imagined Boudu spitting into Balzac? I think not, and the recollection of others confirms this. Something seems to have gone missing here. I guess that one of two things has happened. One is that this was the scene that shocked the original audiences, more than Boudu's eating sardines with his fingers or wiping off the polish from his hands on Madame Lestingois' bedclothes, and it was cut. The other is that projectionists cut it out for their own and their friends' enjoyment. This also often happened. The film virtually disappeared for about twenty years before and after the war. Perhaps I was lucky and saw a rare original at the Cinémathèque in Paris in the early 1960s. At any rate the scene seems to have gone. Sesonske's detailed account of the film seems to confirm that there is a missing spitting-in-the-book scene.

In quick succession Boudu gooses Anne-Marie, swings from the door lintel, and flirts with Anne-Marie, who says she *might* let him kiss her if he shaves his beard. He takes scissors and cuts off half of it (more contrary behaviour). He is told to go to the barber but before he goes out he must clean his shoes. There then follows mayhem in which he destroys the kitchen, leaves the taps running, wipes the shoe polish on Madame Lestingois' bedspread, and does a handstand.

When he returns from the barber it is a different Boudu, walking with an insolent swagger. Now he really could walk along the Bois de Boulogne with an independent air and the people would stop and stare and he'd hear them all declare, he's a millionaire, the man who broke the bank at Monte Carlo. Well, he's about to win the lottery.

He sings Anne-Marie's song, and Anne-Marie is clearly falling for him. Barely literate, Boudu fancies himself as Lestingois' partner as a bookseller. He stands in the doorway of the bookshop and tells a would-be customer who wants Baudelaire's *Les Fleurs du mal* that this is not a flower-shop.

When Lestingois discovers that Boudu has spat in the Balzac, he is as annoyed as such a mild-mannered man can be. It was a magnificent

edition, and Boudu has insulted literature. He tells Boudu he will have to mend his ways. And Madame Lestingois wants to give him a proper talking to about the shoe polish and the kitchen wreckage. Boudu goes off with a jaunty air. He doesn't just call her *tu* (she calls him *vous*), he calls her 'Emma', something even her husband rarely does. He refuses to discuss his misdemeanours or anything other than the mole on her left breast. He embraces her and then not so much falls into bed with her as onto her in the bed – falling, in fact, out of the bottom of the frame. An unseen Mme Lestingois gives a pleasured moan of 'Boudu', while the camera moves to the wall on which hangs an Image d'Epinal (these inexpensive hand-coloured prints were immensely popular at the time). This one is of a young man in uniform playing a cornet. Is this a pun? Lestingois has been cuckolded; he has horns. We are looking at a picture of a horn-player. The pun doesn't work so well in French, so is probably not intended.

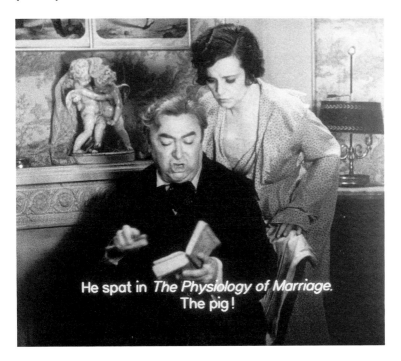

He spat in *The Physiology of Marriage.*
The pig!

Through the window comes the sound of horns playing in the street; the trombone and trumpet and drums of the procession announcing that Lestingois has been awarded a decoration for saving the life of the man who has just given him horns.

Madame gets up from the bed. For the first time in the film she has an expression of pleasure. From now on she is a different person. It's not long before we see her in a polka-dot dress, and she is evidently eager to repeat her experience with Boudu. The incidents follow quickly. Lestingois has been decorated. Boudu wins 100,000 francs in the lottery. In a Feydeau-like scene, Anne-Marie and Lestingois are found in each other's arms at the same time as are Boudu and Madame.

This scandalous situation presents a problem in a respectable household, a household where they have a piano which no one plays. Boudu has the solution in the form of the lottery money. Boudu has the dowry, marriage to Anne-Marie is the answer. It looks as though a *ménage à quatre* is in prospect. This is confirmed in the next scene, a wedding party in the rowing-boat, where Lestingois reads out a little speech in which he says, 'Let us bless the good fortune which, in the form of a lottery ticket, allows carefree youth and innocent beauty to join together.'

'For once,' he goes on, 'we have been able to conform to the morals of the time and respect the laws of divine nature.' Then he spouts some flowery stuff about Priapus Boudu and Chloé Anne-Marie, and he is safely back in the romantic pastoralism with which the film began. It is Lestingois' way of keeping reality at a distance. Morality too, perhaps.

To the sound of 'The Blue Danube' from the violins on the bank, the party in the boat flows happily on. There's the Lestingois husband and wife, Boudu and Anne-Marie, the flautist neighbour and the other neighbour who recommended Lestingois for a decoration, and – unless I'm mistaken (if it isn't Jean Dasté, it looks very much like him) – the student to whom Lestingois gave the Voltaire. And they really do look happy, even Madame Lestingois, who smiles contentedly. Boudu has an idiotic grin on his face. He is in conventional wedding attire, wearing a bowler hat.

Now we're out of the Fauchois play and into pure Renoir, and Renoir is never purer than when in his element, water. These last minutes of the film are simply beautiful. There is a long water shot, into which dips the blade of an oar. To the strains of Strauss the wedding party in the little boat smile their own smiles, thinking their own contented thoughts. Boudu sees a water-lily (remarkably like one of Monet's), reaches out to pick it and capsizes the boat. The others swim for the shore with cries of 'Boudu! Boudu! Boudu-u-u! BOUDU!'

Boudu just floats away on his back, looking at one point very much like a parody of Millais' pre-Raphaelite 'Death of Ophelia'. And then he rolls over and swims. Boudu *can swim*! He might not have drowned even without Lestingois' help – except that he wanted to drown.

André Bazin, in his book on Renoir, is particularly perceptive about these last scenes. When Boudu upsets the boat,

> Dramatic or psychological logic would demand that such an act have a precise meaning. Is it despair, suicide? Probably not, but it

Boudu in wedding attire

is at least an attempt at escape. Boudu is fleeing the chains of a bourgeois marriage. This interpretation, although more ambiguous, would still lend a certain meaning to the shot. Boudu's fall would remain an *act*. But Renoir, like his character, quickly forgets the *act* in favour of the *fact*, and the true object of the scene ceases gradually to be Boudu's intentions and becomes rather the spectacle of his pleasure and, by extension, the enjoyment that Renoir derives from the antics of his hero. The water is no longer 'water' but more specifically the water of the Marne in August, yellow and glaucous. Michel Simon floats on it, turns over, sprays like a seal; and as he plays we begin to perceive the depth, the quality, even the tepid warmth of that water.

Once on dry land Boudu shakes himself dry like a dog. 'The Blue Danube' is now being played by plucked guitar, violin and piano. Boudu walks down a lane and sees a scarecrow. As the music takes up an ever more triumphant rhythm, Boudu pulls the scarecrow out of the ground and carries it on his back, its outstretched arms making him look very much like Christ carrying the cross. He exchanges his wedding clothes for those of the scarecrow.

He walks along the towpath and passes a picnicking couple who give him a sausage to eat. Boudu says, 'I can't eat this without bread.' Boudu's himself again, ungrateful and honest as ever, the man who

The water lily   Boudu's hat

never said thank you to anyone. They give him some bread, which we next see him sharing with a goat. He rolls on his back, half-animal once more.

We hear the long factory siren, a mournful howl from the workaday world. Boudu throws his bowler hat in the water. Now a harmonica very gently plays 'Sur les bords de la Riviera'. The camera lingers for a while on the hat floating on the water and then starts on what Bazin calls 'an extraordinary slow 360-degree pan [which] shows us the countryside he sees before him'.

In fact it is a good bit less than 360 degrees, but Bazin is right in saying that it is extraordinary. I disagree, though, when he says that it shows the intrinsic beauty of the banks of the Marne. This is an industrial landscape, at least on the opposite bank, which is the one Boudu and the camera are looking at. Then, Bazin writes,

> At the end of the pan, the camera picks up a bit of grass where, in close-up, one can see distinctly the white dust that the heat and the wind have lifted from the path. One can almost feel it between one's fingers. Boudu is going to stir it up with his foot. If I were deprived of the pleasure of seeing *Boudu* again for the rest of my days, I would never forget that grass, that dust, and their relationship to the liberty of a tramp.

I have repeatedly searched but in vain: I can't find this detail in the film. If it has been lost it's a great pity. Bazin did not have the benefit of a video with freeze and replay as we do. If Bazin imagined it, then it is to his credit. His description is a lovely piece of writing and it captures the essential quality of the scene to perfection.

On the bank is the Boudu-less wedding party, Lestingois with Anne-Marie leaning on one shoulder, his wife on the other, his arms around them both. 'Where is Boudu?' Anne-Marie asks. Lestingois replies, 'It is his destiny. He is following the current again.' ('*Il a repris le fil de l'eau*'.) Once more it is Renoir *père*'s cork on the stream.

And then the final shot of a procession of tramps, seen from below, against the sky with Sainte-Chapelle (or is it the spire of Notre Dame?) in the background. They are chanting 'Sur les bords de la Riviera'.

Dans le bleu jusqu'au firmament
Les violins jettent leur mélopée
Tous les mots sont plus doux
Plus nombreux les serments
C'est l'amener [l'amour?] qui nous aime [aide?] en chantant.

Why do the tramps sing about the firmament? Why do pictures of church buildings punctuate the film and now provide the final image? The camera points up at the sky, so we must suppose that it is directed at heaven. And in this thoroughly secular film, what is the significance of the inescapably Christ-like appearance of Boudu as he carries the scarecrow? I can't answer these questions. In fact, every time I watch the film I notice something more which I can't quite explain.

I doubt if Renoir could have explained it all. It doesn't matter, any more than the anatomical impossibilities in some of the very greatest

With the scarecrow

paintings matter, or the confused plots of some of Shakespeare's plays. All that matters is that the details work in their context, and that the thing works as a whole. *Boudu* works superbly. André Bazin puts it like this:

> A fraction of these 'mistakes' would condemn any other director. But they are an integral part of the style of Jean Renoir, often the best part of it. For Renoir, what is important is not the dramatic part of a scene. . . . It is sufficient to sketch just enough of it so that the audience has the satisfaction of understanding. That done, the real film remains to be made: characters, objects, light, all must be arranged in the story like colours in a drawing, without being directly subordinated to it. At times the very interest of the finished product may be in the fact that the colours do not fit neatly within the contours of the drawing. The effects

With the goat

Renoir creates out of this overlapping seem all the more subtle because he knows how to stay within the lines beautifully when he wants to.

. . . .

A little more archaeology, sedimentology or searching of sources. I said I was puzzled as to the significance (if any) of the fact that at the end of the film, when Simon walks with the scarecrow on his back, it looks as though he is carrying a crucifix. He then changes his wedding clothes with the rags of the scarecrow. Some weeks after I had written those words, something stirred in the back of my mind which sent me back far beyond Fauchois or Shaw or Smollett or even Shakespeare.

And after that they had mocked him, they took the robe off from him, and put his own raiment on him, and led him away to crucify him. And as they came out, they found a man of Cyrene, Simon by name: him they compelled to bear his cross. (Matthew 27: 31–32.)

Is there a sly, private joke here, between Renoir and Simon? It doesn't matter. What matters is that those final moments of *Boudu* are lovely, some of the loveliest ever to have graced the screen.

10

. . . .

The river flows on. The Michel Simon tramp figure at the end of *La Chienne*, continued as Boudu, completes the trilogy in Jean Vigo's *L'Atalante*. From the wedding scene and village at the end of *Boudu* we seem to flow naturally into the beginning of Vigo's film. Again there is a wedding, and boats and water, and again Simon, but he is older now, Père Jules, and the atmosphere is altogether darker.

For an account of this magical film I refer the reader to Marina Warner's volume in this series. I would just add an idea for discussion about the character of Père Jules. If Lestingois and Boudu are a pair of complementary characters linked by their differences – nature versus culture, intellect against instinct – in Père Jules they are brought together in a single character. He is often thoroughly Boudu-ish (as in the extraordinary scene when he wrestles with himself, or when he appears to smoke a cigarette which is held in his navel). At the same time Vigo–Simon's Père Jules also has an intellect. He is skilful with his gramophone and other mechanical devices. He has travelled all over the world. Like Lestingois he is a collector. His tattooed body must be counted a work of art. He is kind, he is thoughtful, he pulls people out of the water both physically and emotionally.

Legrand in *La Chienne* was in succession a humble clerk, a great painter, a murderer and a tramp. In *Boudu*, the attributes are divided between Lestingois and Boudu. In Père Jules they are brought together in one character. His cabin is like a magician's cell, inhabited by Prospero and Caliban in one body.

Renoir's influence on the subsequent development of the art of cinema has been enormous. Orson Welles and Truffaut both said that Renoir was the greatest of all film directors, and *Boudu* is one of his best films (for me *the* best). It virtually vanished from sight for a long period during and after the war, which is the only possible explanation for its not being far better known. Even so, among Renoir's films *Boudu* specifically has had its inheritors.

One, I think, is the films of Roman Polanski. Polanski was a semi-French student at the Lodz film school in Poland, and as such clearly had a good knowledge of cinema history. His first short film was *Two Men and a Wardrobe* (1958). The two men emerge from the water carrying a wardrobe, wander around, fail to find a home for it, and return with it back into the water. This little fable seems to have at least a germ of *Boudu* in it.

Polanski's first feature-length film was the 1962 *Knife in the Water*. Polanski's unnamed young man, like Boudu, is a vagrant. In an apparent suicide bid he stands in front of an oncoming car and is saved by the quick reactions of the driver, Andrzej, a wealthy man who takes him on to his yacht with his wife Christine. Boudu's attempted suicide was in the water and he is given shelter on dry land; with Polanski's vagrant it is the other way round. Andrzej is not only rich and cultured but also condescending. He teaches the young man various sailing skills, table manners and even instructs him in morality. The young man responds with Boudu-like athleticism (climbing the mast), and indifference to the norms and aspirations of the professional class. He also makes love with Andrzej's wife. There are a number of other similarities, including a fake drowning (and also the virtuoso camerawork, especially of water), and at the end the vagrant goes back on the road.

It is a brilliant film, but the comparison is not to Polanski's advantage. Where Renoir's relationship with his characters is one of warmth, empathy and sympathy, Polanski's is cold and unfeeling. If he doesn't care for them, why should we?

Very different is Paul Mazursky's *Down and Out in Beverly Hills* (1986), which explicitly credits *Boudu* – not Renoir's film but Fauchois' play. This is strange because there are many details in the American film which are straight from Renoir and not to be found in Fauchois (the lost dog, among others). It doesn't really matter who the credit goes to, because *Down and Out* changes everything, turning it into a sometimes rather heavy-handed social comedy on rich West Coast nutters.

A more important change is in the central character. Where Boudu is threatening, Jerry is charming. In fact he turns out to be an articulate, super-intelligent, multi-talented polymath. The plot goes off in all directions in a hyperactive way which is quite amusing, but Jerry's role in it becomes less that of Boudu than that of Père Jules in *L'Atalante*, a kind of fairy godfather who sorts out everyone else's emotional problems.

I have argued against the simplistic idea that Renoir toughened the conventional romantic ending of Fauchois' play. Certainly he changed it, but neither version has such an ending. Fauchois' play ends on a tone of 'And so they got married and lived *un*happily ever after'. In the film Boudu escapes marriage, drifts with the stream and returns to his old life, preferring vagabondage to bondage. Renoir's is much closer to being a happy ending – in fact the closing shot, camera pointing up at the sky, is in every sense uplifting.

It has been so generally accepted (contrary to the evidence) that the Fauchois play had a happy ending that it seems as though there was an unconscious wish for such a version to exist. And doesn't *Down and Out in Beverly Hills* come up with it? Small children make more convincing shows of running away from home than Jerry does. Big, brave, *wise* Jerry *doesn't even make it to the end of the road* before he comes back to the bosom of the family (bosoms, indeed) to resume his life as parasite on a millionaire host. Jerry has admitted that his heartbreak tales of unhappy love and a sister who died of leukaemia were all lies. When Jerry returns to the fold he shows that everything about him is a lie, and there isn't a dry eye in the place. It is just such a morally fraudulent ending that both Fauchois and Renoir (in their different ways) avoided.

The best thing in *Down and Out* is the dog Matisse, who steals scene after scene. Dogs do, as Shakespeare learnt early on, since the only real dog on his stage is in what is probably his first play, *The Two Gentlemen of Verona*. It is the cause of what is for me Shakespeare's best comic monologue. It also anticipates *Boudu* (the *Boudu* of Jean Renoir and Michel Simon) in extraordinary detail. It's not just that the dog Crab is as errant as Black, or that Lance saved him from drowning, it's also that when Lance addresses Crab it could be Lestingois talking to Boudu after he has flooded the kitchen, wiped his shoes on the satin and spat in the Balzac: a Lestingois who by the standards of that good-natured man is *very angry indeed*, but unable to control his affection. Renoir is as close to Shakespeare as anyone in the brief history of the cinema. Here they are in sync.

Enter Lance and his dog Crab

LANCE (*to the audience*): When a man's servant shall play the cur with him, look you, it goes hard. One that I brought up of a puppy, one that I saved from drowning when three or four of his blind brothers and sisters went to it. I have taught him, even as one would say precisely 'Thus I would teach a dog'. I was sent to deliver him as a present to Mistress Silvia from my master, and I came no sooner into the dining-chamber but he steps me to her trencher and steals her capon's leg.

O, 'tis a foul thing when a cur cannot keep himself in all companies. I would have, as one should say, one who takes upon him to be a dog indeed, to be, as it were, a dog at all things. If I had not had more wit than he, to take a fault upon me that he did,

I think verily he had been hang'd for't. Sure as I live, he had suffered for't.

You shall judge. He thrusts me himself into the company of three or four gentleman-like dogs under the Duke's table. He had not been there – bless the mark – a pissing-while but all the chamber smelt him. 'Out with the dog,' says one. 'What cur is that?' says another. 'Whip him out,' says the third. 'Hang him up,' says the Duke.

I, having been acquainted with the smell before, knew it was Crab, and goes me to the fellow that whips the dogs. 'Friend,' quoth I, 'You mean to whip the dog.' 'Ay, marry do I,' quoth he. 'You do him the more wrong,' quoth I, ''twas I did the thing you wot of.' He makes no more ado, but whips *me* out of the chamber.

How many masters would do this for his servant? Nay, I'll be sworn I have sat in the stocks for puddings he hath stolen, otherwise he had been executed. I have stood on the pillory for geese he hath killed, otherwise he had suffered for't. (*To Crab*) Thou think'st not of this now. Nay, I remember the trick you served me when I took my leave of Madam Silvia. Did I not bid thee still mark me, and do as I do? When didst thou see me heave up my leg and make water against a gentlewoman's farthingale? Did'st thou ever see me do such a trick?

It's as bad as spitting in the Balzac.

Author's note: My personal preference for the possessive in names ending with s is, for example, Jones's rather than Jones'. Therefore I would rather have had Fauchois's and Lestingois's, but this does not conform with the BFI house-style.

NOTES

· ·

1 Guy de Maupassant, *A Day in the Country and other stories*, translated and edited by David Coward (London: Oxford University Press, 1990).

2 'Vaudeville' doesn't sound right. In French the word means something more like 'farce', whereas vaudeville in English is music hall. If this is a bad translation, it is not the only one in a book which at one point refers to Picasso wearing 'a melon-coloured hat', which can only be a mistranslation of 'un chapeau melon', a bowler hat. François Truffaut, *The Films in My Life*, trans. Leonard Mayhew (Harmondsworth: Penguin, 1982).

3 An equally bizarre coincidence is the shot at the end of *Boudu* where the boat rowed across the river is the same boat and with the same rower, Georges Darnoux, as in *Une Partie de campagne*, made four years later.

4 Shaw's punctuation.

5 In *An Anatomy of Laughter* (London: Collins, 1974).

CREDITS

· ·

Boudu sauvé des eaux

France
1932
Production company
Les Productions Michel
Simon with the participation
of CCF
French premiere
11 November 1932
UK release
1965
UK distributor
Contemporary
US release
1967
US distributor
Pathé Contemporary

Producer
Michel Simon
Production managers
Jean Gehret, Marc Le
Pelletier
Unit manager
Clément Ollier
Director
Jean Renoir
Assistant directors
Jacques Becker, (Georges
Darnoux)
Screenplay
Jean Renoir, from the play
by René Fauchois
Lighting
Marcel Lucien
**Photography (black and
white)**
(Georges) Asselin
Music
title and end music by
Raphael
flute music by J. Boulze
orphéon music by Edouard
Dumoulin
'The Blue Danube' by
Johann Strauss
Editors
Suzanne de Troeye,
(Marguerite Houllé-Renoir)
Decors
(Hugues) Laurent, (Jean)
Castanier
Sound
(Igor B.) Kalinowski
87 minutes
7,830 ft
Available on VHS in the UK
on the Artificial Eye label

Michel Simon
Boudu
Marcelle Hainia
Mme Lestingois
Séverine Lerczinska
Anne-Marie
Jean Gehret
Vigour
Max Dalban
Godin
Jean Dasté
Student
Charles Granval
M. Lestingois
Jacques Becker
Poet on park bench
Jane Pierson
Rose
Georges Darnoux
A wedding guest
Régine Lutèce
A passer-by

Credits compiled by Markku
Salmi. Names in brackets
are from sources other than
the credits on the screen.

BIBLIOGRAPHY
. . . .

André Bazin, *Jean Renoir* (Paris: Edition Champ Libre, 1971).

Ronald Bergan, *Jean Renoir: projections of paradise* (London: Bloomsbury, 1992).

Celia Bertin, *Jean Renoir* (Paris: Librairie Académique Perrin, 1986).

Claire Blakeway, *Jacques Prévert: popular French theatre and cinema* (London: Associated University Presses, 1990).

Richard Boston, *An Anatomy of Laughter* (London: Collins, 1974).

Leo Braudy, *Jean Renoir: The world of his films* (New York: Doubleday, 1972).

Pierre Braunberger, *Cinémamémoires* (Paris: Editions du Centre Pompidou et Centre National de la Cinématographie, 1987).

Armand-Jean Cauliez, *Jean Renoir* (Paris: Editions Universitaires, 1962).

Frank Curot, *Jean Renoir: L'eau et la terre dans les films de Jean Renoir* (Paris: Minard, 1990).

Raymond Durgnat, *Jean Renoir* (London: Studio Vista, 1975).

Jacques Fanston, *Michel Simon* (Paris: Seghers, 1970).

Christopher Faulkner, *The Social Cinema of Jean Renoir* (Princeton University Press, 1986).

Claude Gauteur, 'Boudu sauvé des eaux de Fauchois à Renoir', *Images et Son*, no. 184, May 1965.

Penelope Gilliatt, *Jean Renoir* (New York: McGraw-Hill, 1975).

Pauline Kael, *5001 Nights at the Movies* (New York: Holt, Rinehart and Winston, 1982).

André Klopmann, *Michel Simon* (Geneva: Editions de l'unicorne, 1993).

Claudio Magriz, *Danube* (London: Collins Harvill, 1989).

Gerald Mast, *The Comic Mind: comedy and the movies* (Indianapolis/New York: Bobbs-Merrill, 1973).

Janice Morgan, 'From Clochards to Cappuccinos: Renoir's Boudu is "Down and Out" in Beverly Hills', *Cinema Journal* 29, no. 2, Winter 1990.

Jean Renoir, *Renoir, My Father* (London: Collins, 1962).

Jean Renoir, *Ma Vie et mes films* (Paris: Flammarion, 1974; trans. as *My Life and My Films* by Norman Denny, New York: Atheneum, 1974).

Jean Renoir, *Ecrits 1926–1971* (Paris: Belfond, 1974).

Jean Renoir, *Renoir on Renoir: Interviews, Essays and Remarks*, trans. Carol Volk (Cambridge: Cambridge University Press, 1989).

Alexander Sesonske,

Jean Renoir: the French Films (Cambridge, MA: Harvard University Press, 1980).

François Truffaut, *The Films in My Life*, trans. Leonard Mayhew (Harmondsworth: Penguin, 1982).

ALSO PUBLISHED

L'Atalante Marina Warner
A splendid job of evoking this very special
film's very special atmosphere.
Empire

The Big Heat Colin MacArthur
Recommended.
Sunday Times

Blackmail Tom Ryall
Ryall catches interestingly that moment
when everyone thought talkies were a
passing fad, and digs up some great quotes.
Empire

Brief Encounter Richard Dyer

Citizen Kane Laura Mulvey
... Ranks among the best things ever written
about the movie.
Film Review

Double Indemnity Richard Schickel
A fine account of Billy Wilder's struggle to
adapt James M. Cain's hard-boiled novel for
the screen.
Time Out

42nd Street J. Hoberman
A rarity: a book written with enough
enthusiasm to make you want to watch the
film again.
Empire

Greed Jonathan Rosenbaum
(A) brilliantly researched account of the
making of Erich von Stroheim's 1923
masterpiece.
Film Review
A very readable introduction to the film and
its fascinating and complicated history.
Movie Collector

In a Lonely Place Dana Polan
The film is still underrated, and Polan makes
a powerful case for taking it out of its cult
noir slot and installing it as a major classic.
Empire

It's a Gift Simon Louvish

Olympia Taylor Downing
Downing does a fascinating job,
documenting the problematic production and
showing how the director played off her
personal friendship with Hitler to get it done
at all.
Empire

Rocco and his Brothers Sam Rohdie

The Seventh Seal Melvyn Bragg

Singin' in the Rain Peter Wollen
Fascinating.
Time Out

Stagecoach Edward Buscombe
A hugely entertaining account of the film's
making.
Film Review

Went the Day Well? Penelope Houston
The strength of the best Anglo-Saxon
tradition of film criticism – finely crafted and
intellectually rigorous – is discernible on
each page ...
The Times Saturday Review

Wizard of Oz Salman Rushdie
Witty and vivacious ... shrewd and joyous
... it adds to the movie's wonder, which is
saying a lot.
New Statesman & Society
... his finest piece of writing since his
withdrawal from everyday life.
London Review of Books

**If you would like further information
about future BFI Film Classics or about
other books on film, media and popular
culture from BFI Publishing, please write
to:**

**BFI Film Classics
British Film Institute
21 Stephen Street
London
W1P 1PL**